NEW DIMENSIONS IN TATTING

Colour photo 1   A variety of flowers and leaves

NEW DIMENSIONS IN TATTING

New approaches to an old technique

To de Haan-van Beek

Kangaroo Press

PUBLISHER'S NOTE:

The author's reference to tatting with a needle beginning on page 40 is quite different from modern needle tatting as is practised today. The author uses the needle in lieu of a shuttle to manipulate the thread in the traditional manner. In modern needle tatting the knots are formed directly on the needle eliminating the knot transfer of traditional tatting.

All patterns and techniques developed in this book can be easily worked by the popular modern needle tatting technique. Reference is made to *The Complete Book of Tatting* by Rebecca Jones and *Needle Tatting* by Barbara Foster for those unfamiliar with needle tatting basics.

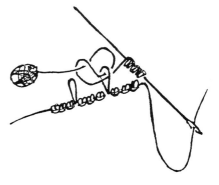

To work the novel 'inverted tatting' as shown in diagram 14.2, using needle tatting technique, refer to figure to the right. Work one half the ring in the normal manner forming the first 4 picots on the needle. Pull needle through as you would for a chain and work again on the needle the first joining picot in the normal manner. Make the joining by pulling a loop of the ball thread through the connecting picot and then pull the ball thread through this just formed loop. Pull taut and continue tatting in the normal manner.

Photography: Maarijn ten Holt, Zuiderwoude
Drawings: Katja Nootenboom, IJsselstein
English translation: Tina Llowarch

Translated from the Dutch title
KLEURRIJK FRIVOLITE
Originally published by
Cantecleer bv, de Bilt
© 1982 Uitgeverij Cantecleer bv, de Bilt

© English text Kangaroo Press 1994

This edition first published in 1994
by Kangaroo Press Pty Ltd
3 Whitehall Road Kenthurst NSW 2156
PO Box 6125 Dural Delivery Centre NSW 2158
Typeset by G.T. Setters Pty Limited
Printed in Singapore by Kyodo Printing Co. (S'pore) Pte Ltd

ISBN 0 86417 599 X

Contents

I Introduction

The aim of this book is firstly to introduce the technique of tatting to the beginner. With the basic information given here, the beginner can become proficient in the art of the new coloured tatting. More experienced tatters will also find a lot of new information.

In recent years renewed interest has been shown in the art of tatting in many countries, with a number of different publications returning the art to public view. This interest is displayed by young and old. Older people can probably remember displays of tatting at craft shows, where often very beautiful pieces could be admired. Younger people may be fascinated by a very cost effective craft which can achieve brilliant results, giving a very personal finish to clothing or interior decorating, for example.

How old is the art of tatting? There seems to be quite a difference of opinion here. Some say it began in Western Europe in the sixteenth century, others say it is much older than that. It is a fact, however, that tatting has been practised in Europe for several centuries. As in many aspects concerning the lives of our forefathers we have gained this information from the old paintings of the seventeenth and eighteenth centuries, many of which show clothing decorated with tatted lace and designs.

There are even paintings where women have posed holding tatting tools and cotton in their hands. That tatting was fashionable at that time seems a reasonable conclusion. This seems to have been followed by a lengthy period when there was not much interest in the craft, until at the end of the nineteenth and the beginning of the twentieth centuries tatting came into vogue again. Popular magazines for women at that time featured examples and patterns of tatting. Tatting was featured at craft shows, receiving a lot of attention, and some schools even included classes in tatting in their curriculum.

After World War II the art of tatting was almost forgotten for a long time, but in recent years more and more people have become interested in this old and beautiful craft, in Holland, in most of Europe, in America, Asia and Australia. It is heartening to see this resurgence of interest in an ancient tradition.

This book is intended, with respect for the old tradition, to reveal new possibilities in the art. Through the use of variations to the old shuttle technique and using coloured silks we can achieve results that previously have not been thought possible.

II What is tatting?

In the Netherlands and France the word *frivolité* refers to a certain type of lace, a light, soft delicate, fluffy type of lace. In Germany it is called *Schiffchenspitze*, which can be translated as 'shuttle lace'. It could be said that tatting is a lace made by using shuttles to make it delicate and fragile. On a first inspection the lace may well seem fragile, but all those laces, doilies and collars that were tatted centuries ago and the beautiful flowers and butterflies that are being made nowadays are really quite deceptive in appearance. All tatting in reality has a very strong structure—it is simple, compact and very strong.

The basic structure of tatting is simply a knot, which may not immediately suggest something delicate and fragile. A strong knot, once made, is very difficult to pull apart; the end result of such a solid construction means that tatted pieces are long lasting and need no artificial aid to stay in shape.

Tatting, however, requires a little more than just being able to make knots. It takes some practice to make the knot correctly and a little extra concentration to make several knots and join them with others to form a finished piece.

Put simply, a piece of tatting is formed using one thread which is knotted into rings; the rings are used to make edges, or to form larger rings.

Many variations can be achieved by working with more than one thread to create more intricate patterns and shapes—for example, large collars and hats. In contrast to making lace, tatting requires very few tools—just a few shuttles. If shuttles are not available sewing needles can be used. With a few threads of coloured cotton (and a certain amount of patience) and just a few shuttles or needles, the most intricate designs can be made—for example, flowers, butterflies, a lizard and even a splendid multicoloured tropical fish. Many sources of inspiration for your own designs may be found in nature, in books and magazines and in many other places.

The traditional methods and the lace patterns handed down for many years are still useful. A number of traditional laces and borders have been described in this book but the emphasis is on explaining the many new possibilities of tatting.

III Equipment and materials

Tatting is not an expensive hobby and with the minimal equipment required has the advantage of being easily transportable.

Shuttle

A shuttle is a simple tool, rather like two wings with pointed ends that are joined in the centre (see photo 1). The thread is wound around the joining section. The pointed ends press lightly against each other but are loose enough to let the thread be passed through and strong enough to prevent the thread unravelling while it is being worked. Modern shuttles are usually made of plastic.

There was a time when women who practised the art of tatting used very elaborate and expensive shuttles as a fashion accessory. Some were made of gold and decorated with expensive jewels. Although a tatting shuttle need not be elaborate, some of these shuttles were nonetheless very beautiful.

The simple smooth shuttle available in most craft and hobby shops these days is perfectly suitable. It is a good idea to buy several shuttles, preferably in different colours, to prevent having to switch threads when working with two shuttles.

Crochet hook

The crochet hook is used to join sections of tatting together. Some shuttles have a built-in hook for this purpose, making a separate crochet hook unnecessary. There are different schools of thought on the usefulness of this.

Cotton

In principle you can use many different kinds of thread: crochet cotton, string, wool, embroidery cotton, spliced silk. Whatever you use a thread with a smooth finish is preferable, so that the knots slide along easily when you push them. The thickness of the thread will determine the size of the worked article.

Needle

This may surprise experienced tatters, but later on in this book we will demonstrate that tatting can be refined even further by using a needle rather than a shuttle.

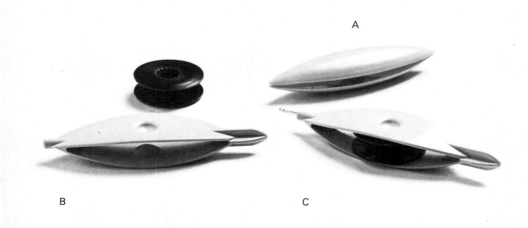

Photo 1   Three shuttles

A.   The classic shuttle
B, C.   Both these shuttles have a removable bobbin which makes it easier to wind the thread. C also has an inbuilt crochet hook

9

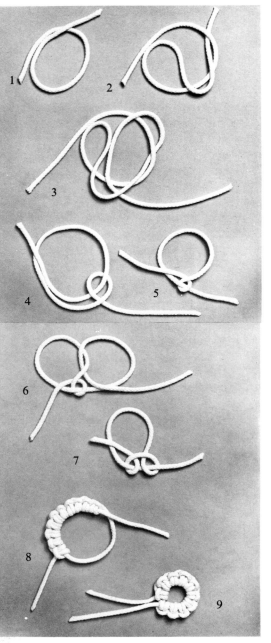

Photo 2 *The basic ring, built up from double knots*

1. Make a loop with the thread
2. The thread (with the shuttle) is passed through the loop
3. The shuttle is passed back over the loop
4. Shuttle thread is loosened and looped thread is tightened
5. Pull looped thread creating the first part of the knot
6. For the second part of the knot, pull the thread through the top of the loop and repeat steps 4 and 5
7. The double knot is complete
8. A number of double knots around the loop
9. Pull the loop and close the ring

IV The technique

As explained previously, the basis of tatting is a knot. The knot consists of two parts and is thus called a double knot. Tatting does not consist entirely of knots, but also includes picots, created by leaving a space between the knots.

Some people will find it easy to use the shuttle when they get started, others may need to persevere for a while. But don't be disheartened if you find it difficult at first—practice will get you there. The photos from here to page 20 will help you master the art of tatting.

The basic ring

The basic ring, built up with double knots, is shown in photos 2.1 to 2.9. The result is a circle. Photos 3.1 to 3.12 show how the basic ring can be made using a shuttle.

Before you go any further it is advisable to practise these circles until you are able to make the knots without difficulty. If the thread starts to twist while you are working let the shuttle dangle from the thread and untwist itself.

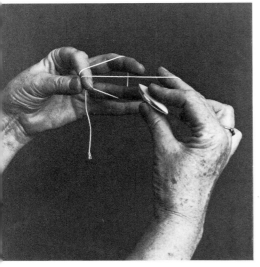

Photo 3.1   Loop the thread around the fingers of the left hand, holding the shuttle in the right hand

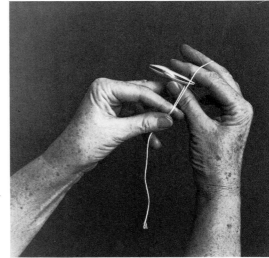

Photo 3.2   The shuttle is passed through the loop around the fingers of the left hand

11

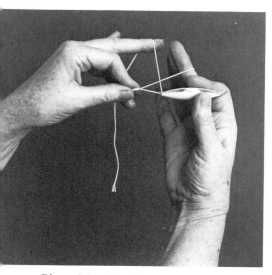 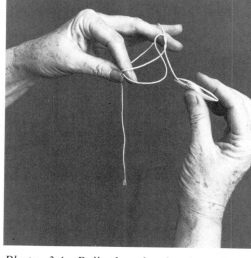

Photo 3.3   Pass the shuttle back over the loop, thereby tightening the loop

Photo 3.4   Pull the shuttle through further, which will cause the loop and the thread to loosen

Photo 3.5   Keeping the shuttle thread loose, tighten the loop in the left hand

Photo 3.6   Pull the loop firmly, thereby creating the first half of the knot. Tighten the shuttle thread. The knotting is done with the loop

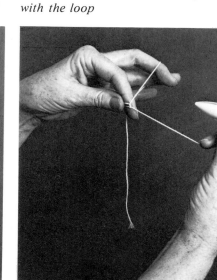

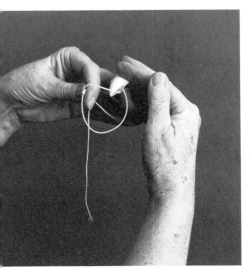

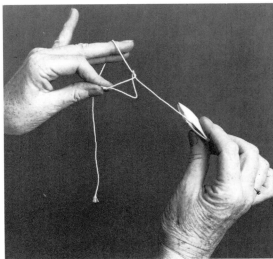

Photo 3.7 The second half of the knot is made by pulling the shuttle through from the top to the lower part of the loop. Hold the knot with the left thumb

Photo 3.8 Pull the shuttle through the loop and release the loop

Photo 3.9 Complete the knot by tightening the loop, which also moves the knot along. Keep the shuttle tight

Photo 3.10 The first knot is completed. The knot can be moved backwards and forwards along the shuttle thread

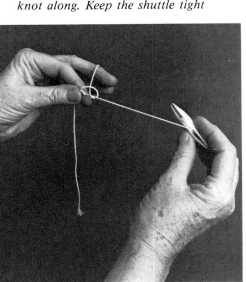

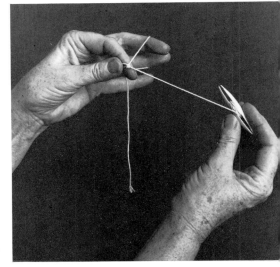

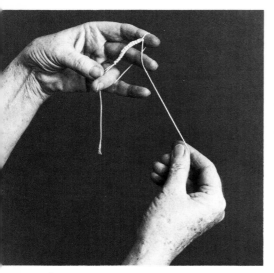

Photo 3.11 *The loop around the hand becomes smaller as more knots are made. With the knots held between thumb and forefinger, gently pull the shuttle thread behind the knots until the loop becomes large enough to fit around the hand again*

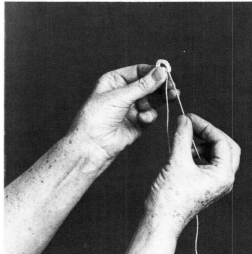

Photo 3.12 *When the number of double knots is sufficient, close the ring*

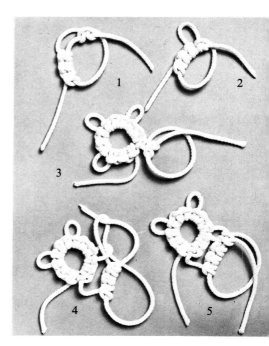

Photo 4 *Joining with picots*

1. The space between the knots indicates the size of the picot
2. The picot is formed by moving the knots along against each other; the space then becomes a picot
3. The second ring with the first double knot
4. The loop has been pulled through the picot of the first circle
5. The two circles are now joined together

Picots

Picots are formed by leaving a space (a length of thread) between the knots. The amount of space determines the size of the picot—see photos 4.1 and 5.1. Pushing the knots together creates the picot—see photos 4.2 and 5.2.

Joining the rings

To join one ring to another you will need to finish the first ring with a picot. A second ring is formed, which is then covered with double knots—see photo 4.3. When you have made three double knots you then pull the loop through the picot of the first ring with a crochet hook—see photo 4.4. Pull the shuttle through the newly formed loop—see photo 4.4. Then tighten the shuttle thread and the loop thread, pulling the knot into position (see photo 4.5) and finish off the second ring.

Photos 5.3 to 5.5 show how picots are made with a shuttle and how to join two rings together. A chain of small rings can be joined up to make a larger ring.

Leaving a small space between the rings on the chain allows a straight edge to develop.

Photo 5.1 Leaving a space between the double knots

Photo 5.2 Pushing the knots together

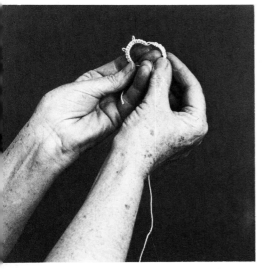

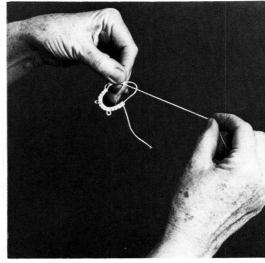

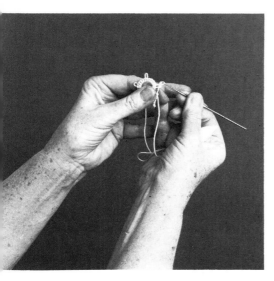

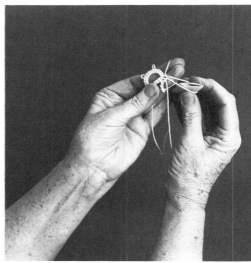

Photo 5.3   Use a crochet hook to pull the loop through the picot

Photo 5.4   Pull the shuttle through the loop

Photo 5.5   Keep the thread taut so that the new knot can be moved along

Photo 6.1   The thread on which the beads are to be threaded is pulled through a folded piece of fuse wire

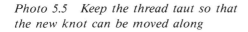

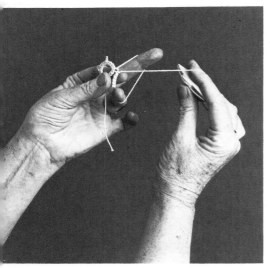

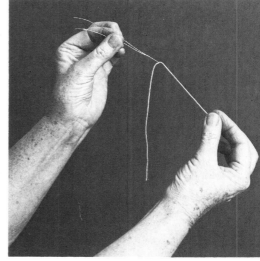

Working with two shuttles or a guide thread

Occasionally a tatting pattern calls for you to make a chain (see lace B, page 22). Chains can be made using either two shuttles or a guide thread. Where beads are used in a pattern they need to be threaded onto a guide thread. Threading small beads is quite easily done by bending a piece of fuse wire around the thread—see photos 6.i and 6.2.

To form a chain you need to reverse the first circle. If this is not done the right hand would have to do the work of the left hand. (In tatting it is usual to work from left to right.)

The second shuttle is held, together with the reversed circle, between the thumb and forefinger—see photo 6.3. (Photos 6.3 to 6.5 actually show a needle being used instead of a shuttle. This is explained in more detail on page 40.)

To make a chain use the guide thread as the picot thread. With the shuttle thread work the knots around the guide thread, close against the circle.

The beads can then be slid along into place between the double knots—see photos 6.4 and 6.5.

Photo 6.2 Using the fuse wire to thread the beads

Photo 6.3 The guide thread is laid next to the reversed circle

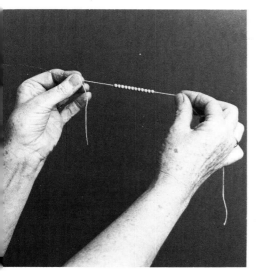

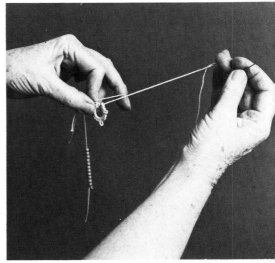

17

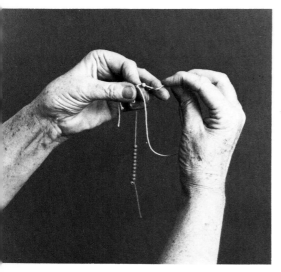

Finishing off

When the tatted piece is completed, finish off with a flat knot—see photos 7.1, 7.2 and 7.3.

Joining a new thread

To join in a new thread, first make a picot in it. Pull the old thread through the picot in the new thread, pushing the picot as close as possible against the work. Pull both ends of the new thread until the old thread is caught up—see photos 7.4 and 7.5.

Photo 6.4   A bead is slid from the guide thread and a double knot is made directly after it

Photo 6.5   This double knot is pushed against the previous knot, positioning the bead at the top of the picot

Photo 7   Finishing off with a flat knot (1 to 3)
Joining a new thread (4 and 5)

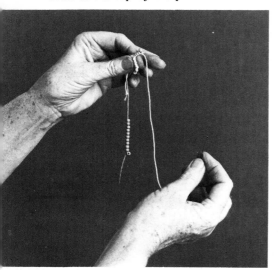

Colour photo 2   A selection of roses and pansies

Abbreviations

The following abbreviations are used throughout the book.

1	Finishing off	Fin
2	Chain	Ch
3	Thread	Th
4	Double knot	DK
5	Reverse work	RW
6	Knot (double)	DK
7	Knotting thread	KT
8	Bead	B
9	Beading thread	BT
10	Beading shuttle	BS
11	Picot	P or −
12	Ring	R
13	Close	Cl
14	Shuttle	Sh
15	Shuttle thread	ST
16	Row	Row
17	Joining	J or +
18	Working thread	WT

Remember − and + (very important in the instructions).

Examples

The number of knots to be made will be indicated by a number.

The instruction:

4 − 4 − 2 − 3 − 3

means:

4 double knots; picot; 4 double knots; picot; 2 double knots; picot; 3 double knots; picot; 3 double knots.

The instruction:

4 − 4 − 2 + (2 P 1 R); 4

means:

4 double knots; picot; 4 double knots; picot; 2 double knots; join with second picot of first ring; 4 double knots.

This instruction for a ring:

R: 2 − 3 − 2 − 3 − 2; R Cl

means:

make the following ring: 2 double knots; picot; 3 double knots; picot; 2 double knots; picot; 3 double knots; picot; 2 double knots; close the ring.

Practising the exercises in this chapter will give you a solid understanding of the basics of tatting. The next chapter contains instructions for four simple laces and four easy decorative pieces for you to start with; later projects are more challenging.

V Laces and simple designs

When you have become familiar with the techniques of knotting and working with two shuttles descibed on pages 10–20, you will be able to make the four laces shown in photo 8.

When you are first learning to tat, don't try to do too much at once. Take a break occasionally; when you get started again things will seem easier.

One of the easier things to start with is a lace that can be used as a decoration for a collar, handkerchief, child's dress or a blouse. Very soon you will move on to a free form of tatting that can be used to make such things as a Christmas star,

Christmas decorations, a fan or a butterfly. I strongly suggest that you follow the order of the book in working pieces rather than start with an example from the back which may require a little more experience. Each example comes with diagrams and corresponding instructions. The heavier lines on the diagrams indicate what is being described in the text.

A straight line represents a *picot*, a circle represents a *ring* and a long curve represents a *chain*.

The starting threads are also clearly marked, so that it is easy to see when the work needs to be reversed.

Photo 8 From left to right: laces A, B, C, D

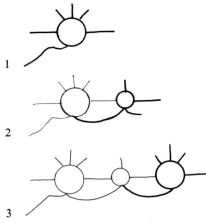

1

2

3

Lace A

Materials: DMC Cotton no. 40 or 50
Equipment: 1 shuttle
Method:
1st R: 3 − 3 − 2 − 2 − 3 − 3; R Cl, see 1.
2nd R: 3 + (5th P 1st R) 3 − 3 − 3: R Cl, see 2.
3rd R: 3 + (3rd P 2nd R) 3 − 2 − 2 − 3 − 3; R Cl, see 3.
4th R: as 2nd R; etc.

1

2

3

4

Lace B

Material: DMC Cotton no. 40 or 50
Equipment: 2 shuttles
Method:
1st Sh; 1st R: 4 − 4 − 2 − 4 − 4; R Cl (P 1 and 4 are larger then P 2 and 3), see 1.
* RW: with 1st Sh onto Th 2nd Sh.
Ch: 3 − 2 − 2 − 2 − 2 − 2 − 2 − 3, see 2.
RW: With 1st Sh; R: 4 + (4th P 1st R) 4 − 2 − 4 − 4; R Cl, see 3.
RW: With 1st Sh; Ch on Th of 2nd Sh: 3 + (7th P 1st Ch) 2 − 2 − 2 − 2 − 3, see 4.
RW: With 1st Sh; R: 4 + (4th P 2nd R) 4 − 2 − 4 − 4; R Cl, see 5.
Repeat from *: after the first 3 DK join the last picot of the previous chain.

5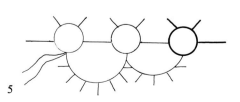

Lace C

Material: DMC Cotton no. 40 or 50
Equipment: 2 shuttles
Method:

1st Sh; R: 6 − 6; R Cl, see 1.
RW: 1st Sh on Th 2nd Sh: 4, see 2.
RW: With 2nd Sh; R: 5 − 7; R Cl, see 3.
* With 1st Sh on Th 2nd Sh: 3, see 4.
With 2nd Sh: R: 6 − 6; R Cl, see 5.
With 1st Sh on Th 2nd Sh: 3, see 6.
With 2nd Sh; R: 7 − 5; R Cl, see 7.
With 1st Sh on Th 2nd Sh: 4, see 8.
RW: With 1st Sh; R: 6 + (1st R) 6 R Cl,
see 9.
RW: With 1st Sh on Th 2nd Sh: 4, see 10
RW: With 1st Sh; R: 6 − 6; R Cl, see 11
RW: with 1st Sh on Th 2nd Sh: 4, see 12
With 2nd Sh; R: 5 + (3rd R) 7; R Cl, see
13.
Repeat from *.

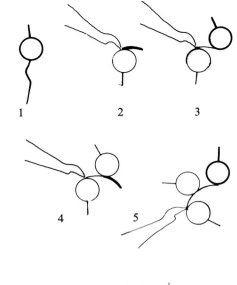

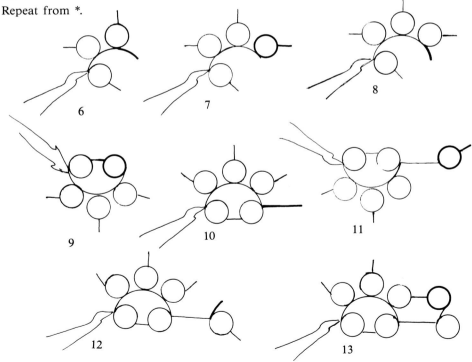

23

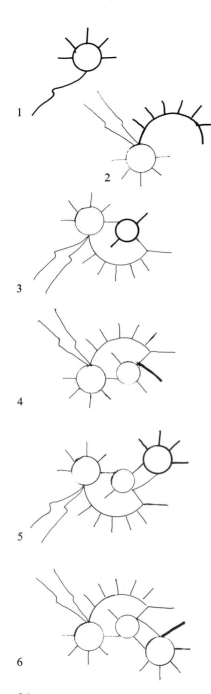

Lace D

Material: DMC Cotton no. 40 or 50
Equipment: 2 Shuttles
Method:
1st Sh; R: 5 − 3 − 2 − 2 − 3 − 5; R Cl, see 1.
* RW: 1st Sh on Th 2nd Sh;
Ch: 3 − 2 − 2 − 2 − 2 − 3 − 4, see 2.
RW: 1st Sh; R: 4 − 4 + (5th P 1st R) 4 − 4; R Cl, see 3.
RW: 1st Sh on Th 2nd Sh; Ch: 4, see 4.
RW: 1st Sh; R: 5 + (3rd P 2nd R) 3 − 2 − 2 − 3 − 5; R Cl, see 5.
RW: With 1st SH on Th 2nd Sh: 4, see 6.
RW: 1st Sh; R: 4 + (5th P 3rd R) 4 − 4 − 4; R Cl, see 7.
RW: With 1st Sh on Th 2nd Sh; Ch: 4 + (6th P 1st Ch) 3 − 2 − 2 — 2 − 2 − 3, see 8.
RW: 1st Sh; R: 5 + (2nd P 4th R) 3 − 2 − 2 − 3 − 5; R Cl, see 9.
Repeat from *.

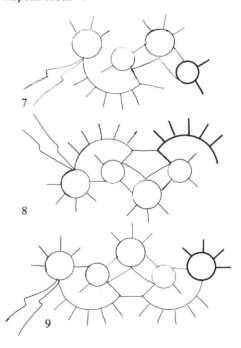

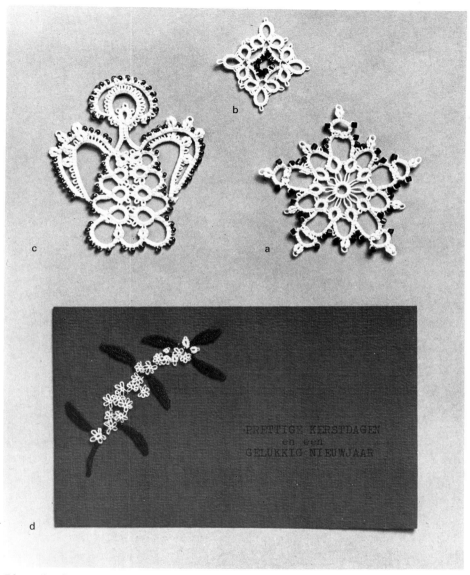

Photo 9   Some simple pieces of tatting

a. *Christmas star (instructions page 26)*
b. *A section of the Christmas decoration in photo 10 on page 28 (instructions page 27)*
c. *Christmas angel (instructions page 46)*
d. *Mistletoe (instructions page 49)*

Christmas star, see photo 9a (page 25)

Material: DMC Cotton no. 40 or 50; 40 small beads

Equipment: 2 shuttles; fine crochet hook no. 12

Method:

Thread the beads as described on page 17. This will be referred to as the beading shuttle.

1st Row: 1st Sh; R: 1 − 2 − 2 − 2 − 2 − 2 − 2 − 2 − 2 − 2 − 1; R Cl; Fin. The first ring is now completed, see 1.

2nd Row: 1st Sh; R: 3 − 3 + (P 1st Row); 3 − 3; R Cl, see 2.

* RW: 1st Sh on BS: 3 − 2 B 2, see 3. Beads are then pushed back; with BS; R: 3 − 3; R Cl, see 4.

1st Sh on BS: 2 B 2 − 3, see 5.

RW: 1st Sh; R: 3 + (1st P R 2nd Row); 3 + (2nd P 1st R); 3 − 3; R Cl. The second ring of the second row is now completed, see 6.

RW: 1st Sh on BS: 3 B 2 B 2, see 7.

RW: 1st Sh; R: 2 − 2; R Cl, see 8

RW: 1st Sh on BS: 2 B 4, see 9.

Beads are pushed back; with BS; R: 3 − 3; R Cl, see 10.

With 1st Sh on BS: 4 B 2, see 11.

RW: 1st Sh; R: 2 + (P from R, diag 8); 2; R Cl, see 12.

RW: 1st Sh on BS: 2 B 2 B 3, see 13.

RW: 1st Sh; R: 3 + (P 2nd R 2nd Row); 3 + (3rd P 1st R); 3 − 3; R Cl, see 14. Repeat from *.

Last R: + (P 1st R 2nd Row).

Starting and ending threads are finished off together.

If desired the finished star could be stiffened with starch or sugar water.

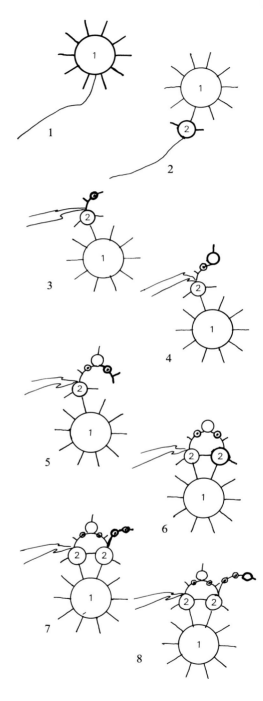

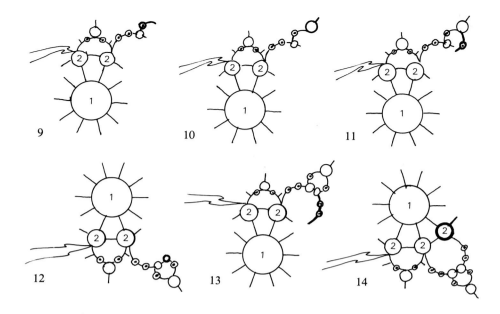

Christmas decoration, see photos 9b (page 25) and 10 (page 28)

Material: DMC Cotton no. 50 or 2 threads of embroidery cotton; 48 small beads; coloured foam ball 5 cm diameter

Equipment: 2 shuttles; crochet hook no. 12

Method:

1st Sh; 1st R: 4 − 4 − 4 − 4; R Cl, see 1.
* 2nd R: 4 + (3rd P 1st R); 7 − 7 − 4; R Cl, see 2.
3rd R: 4 + (last P 2nd R); 4 − 4 − 4; R Cl, see 3.
2nd Sh: thread 48 beads.
RW: with 1st Sh on BS: 3 B 2 B 3, see 4.
RW: 1st Sh; 4 + (last P 3rd R); 4 − 4 − 4; R Cl, see 5.
Repeat from *.
Note: (last P of 12th R) + (1st P 1st R).
Attach the 12 squares around the ball, see 6 on page 28

27

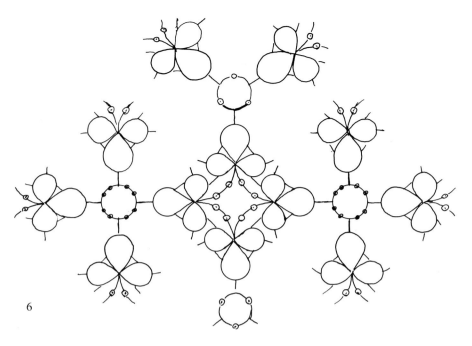

6

*Photo 10 Christmas
decoration*

Colour photo 3   Fuchsias

29

Fan, see photo 11 (page 33)

Materials: DMC Cotton no. 40, white or coloured; 73 small beads

Equipment: 2 shuttles; crochet hook no. 12

Method:

1st R: 1 − 1 − 1 − 1 − 1 − 1 − 5; Fin, see 1.

1st Sh + 1st P; 2nd Sh: thread beads. 1st Sh on BS: 2 B 2 − 2 B 2 − 2 B 2, see 2.

RW: 1st Sh; 2nd R: 3 − 3; R Cl, see 3.

RW: 1st Sh on BS: 2 B 2 − 2 B 2 − 2 B 2, see 4.

RW: 1st Sh; 3rd R: 5 − 5; R Cl, see 5.

RW: 1st Sh on BS: 2 B 2 − 2 B 2 − 2 B 2 − 2 B 2, see 6.

RW: 1st Sh; 4th R: 3 − 2 − 2 − 2 − 3 − 3 − 2 − 2 − 2 − 3; R Cl, see 7.

RW: 1st Sh on BS: 2 B 2 − 2 B 2 − 2 B 2 − 2 B 2 − 2 B 2 − 2 B 2 + (5th P 4th R), see 8.

* 1st Sh on BS: 13 + (P 3rd R) B 11 + (P 2nd R) B 11 + (1st P 1st R), see 9.

1st Sh on BS: 11 + (P 2nd R), see 10.

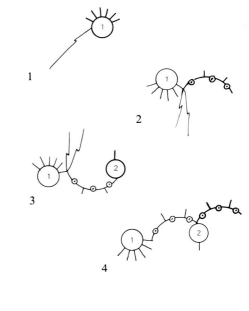

1

2

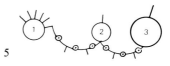

3

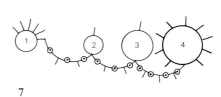

5

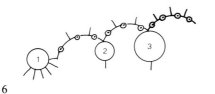

6

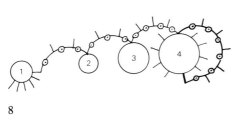

8

7

9

RW: 1st Sh; 2nd R: 3 − 3; R Cl, see 11.
RW: 1st Sh on BS: 11 + (P 3rd R), see 12*.
RW: 1st Sh; 3rd R: 6 − 6; R Cl, see 13.
RW: 1st Sh on BS: 13 + (5th P 4th R), see 14.
RW: 1st Sh; 5th R: 3 − 2 − 2 − 2 − 2 − 2 − 3 − 3 − 2 − 2 − 2 − 2 − 2 − 3; R Cl, see 15.
RW: 1st Sh on BS: 2 − 2 B 2 − 2 B 2 − 2 B 2 − 2 B 2 − 2 B 2 − 2 B 2 + (7th P 5th R), see 16.
Repeat from * to *. *Note:* diagram 9: + (2nd P 1st R).
RW: 1st Sh; 3rd R; 7 − 7; R Cl.
RW: 1st Sh on BS: 13 + (7th P 5th R).

RW: 1st Sh; 6th R: 3 − 2 − 2 − 2 − 2 − 2 − 2 − 3 − 3 − 2 − 2 − 2 − 2 − 2 − 2 − 3.
RW: 1st Sh on BS: 2 − 2 B 2 − 2 B 2 − 2 B 2 − 2 B 2 − 2 B 2 − 2 B 2; + (8th P 6th R), see 17.
Repeat twice (from * to * and diag. 17), respectively join with the 3rd and 4th P of the 1st R (diag. 9), see 18.
As diag. 13; continue 13 DK + (8th P 6th R); diag. 15; diag. 16; diag. 9; diag. 10; diag. 11; diag. 12; diag. 5; then 13 DK + (7th P 5th R); diag. 7; diag. 8; diag. 6 (+ P 3rd R); diag. 4 (+ P 2nd R); diag. 2 (+ last P 1st R), see 18.
RW: 3 B 3 B 5 − 5 − 5 − 14 + (3rd P); 5 + (2nd P); 5 + (1st P); 5 B 3 B 3; thread through (1st P 1st R) pull through back of work; Fin, see 19.

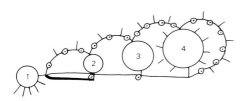

10

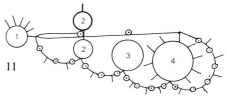

11

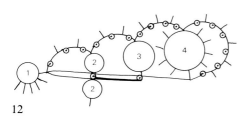

12

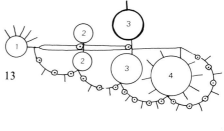

13

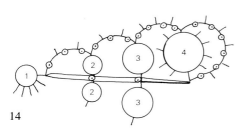

14

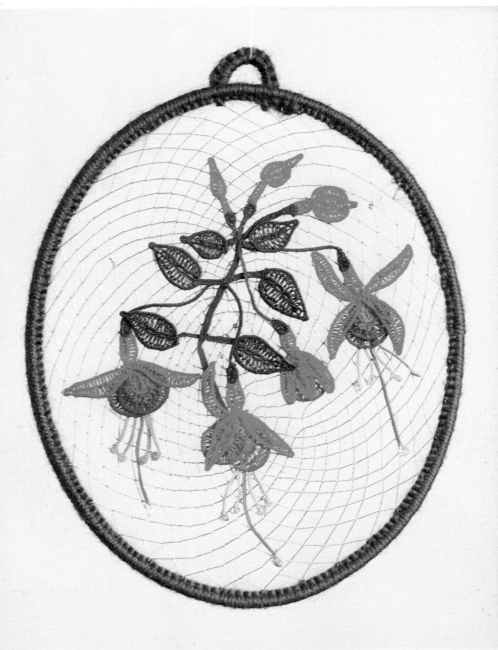

Colour photo 4   Frame with a spray of fuchsias

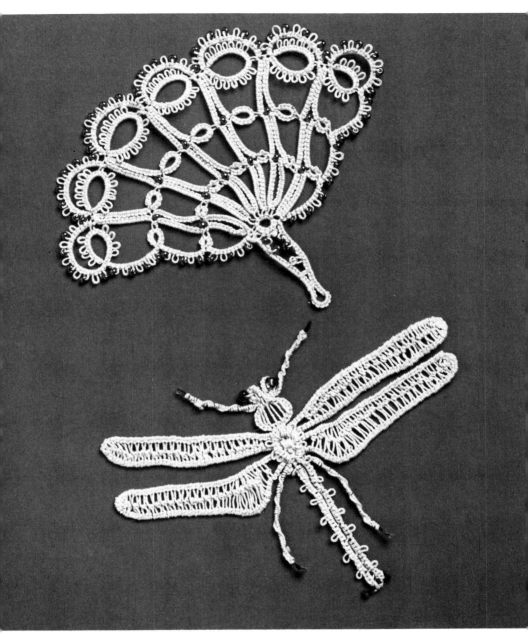

Photo 11   Fan and dragonfly: for instructions see pages 30 and 67

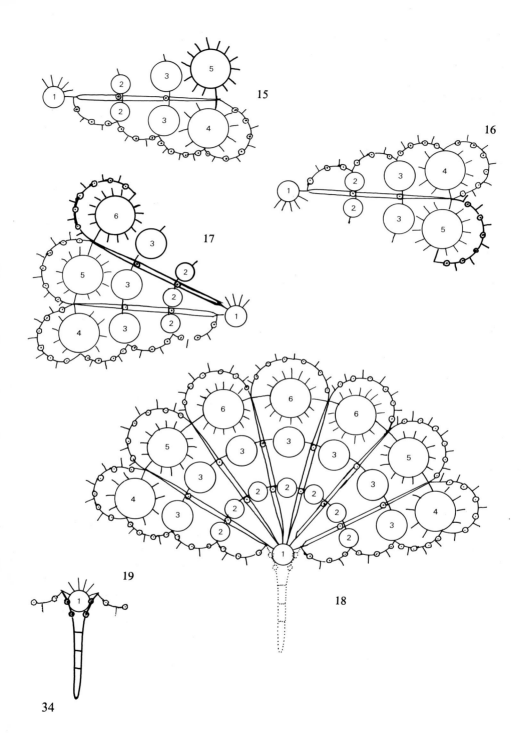

15

16

17

19

18

34

Butterfly, see photo 12 (page 39)

Materials: For the wings, DMC Cotton no. 40, white; for the body DMC Cotton no. 40, white; a thread of thin wool, light brown or beige, approx. 25 cm long; 2 beads

Equipment: 2 shuttles; crochet hook no. 12; darning or embroidery needle; sewing needle no. 8

Worked in similar manner to the fan.

Method:

Lower wing

1st R: 4 − 2 − 2 − 2 − 4; R Cl; 2nd R against 1st R: 4 − 2 − 2 − 2 − 4; R Cl; Fin. and cut thread, see 1.

1st Sh J (1st P R); Ch: 3 − 2 − 2 − 2 − 2;
RW: R: 3 − 3; R Cl;
RW: Ch: 2 − 2 − 2 − 2 − 2 − 2;
RW: R: 5 − 5; R Cl;
RW: Ch: 2 − 2 − 2 − 2 − 2 − 2 − 2;
RW: R: 2 − 2 − 2 − 2 − 2 − 2 − 2 − 2 − 2 − 2; R Cl;
RW: Ch: 2 − 2 − 2 − 2 − 2 − 2 − 2 − 2 − 2 − 2 − 2 + (5th P 4th R);
Ch: 11 + (P 3rd R); 11 + (P 2nd R); 9 + (1st P 1st R);
Ch: 9 + (P between 1st and 2nd Ch);
RW: R: 3 − 3; R Cl;
RW: Ch: 11 + (P between 2nd and 3rd Ch);
RW: R: 6 − 6; R Cl;
RW: Ch: 10 + (P between 3rd and 4th Ch);
RW: R: 2 − 2 − 2 − 2 − 2 − 2 − 2 − 2 − 2 − 2 − 2; R Cl;
RW: Ch: 2 − 2 − 2 − 2 − 2 − 2 − 2 − 2 − 2 − 2 + (6th P 4th R);
Ch: 10 + (P 3rd R); 9 + (P 2nd R); 8 + (2nd P 1st R);
Ch: 8 + (P between 1st and 2nd Ch);
RW: R: 3 − 3; R Cl;
RW: Ch: 9 + (P between 2nd and 3rd Ch);
RW: R: 7 − 7; R Cl;

Ch: 9 + (P between 3rd and 4th Ch);
RW: R: 2 − 2 − 2 − 2 − 2 − 2 − 2 − 2 − 2 − 2 − 2 − 2 − 2 − 2 − 2 − 2 − 2; R Cl;
RW: Ch: 2 − 2 − 2 − 2 − 2 − 2 − 2 − 2 − 2 − 2 − 2 − 2 + (8th P 4th R);
Ch: 7 + (P 3rd R); Ch: 7 + (P 2nd R);
Ch: 8 + (3rd P 1st R);
Ch: 7 + (P between 1st and 2nd Ch);
RW: R: 3 − 3; R Cl;
RW: Ch: 6 + (P between 2nd and 3rd Ch);
RW: R: 7 − 7; R Cl;
RW: Ch: 6 + (P between 3rd and 4th Ch);
RW: R: 2 − 2 − 2 − 2 − 2 − 2 − 2 − 2 − 2 − 2 − 2 − 2 − 2 − 2 − 2 − 2; R Cl;
RW: Ch: 2 − 2 − 2 − 2 − 2 − 2 − 2 − 2 − 2 − 2 − 2 + (8th P 4th R);
Ch: 6 + (P 3rd R);
Ch: 5 + (P 2nd R);
Ch: 6 + (3rd P 1st R); Fin, see 2.

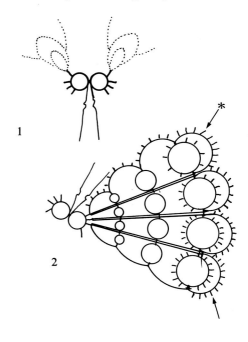

35

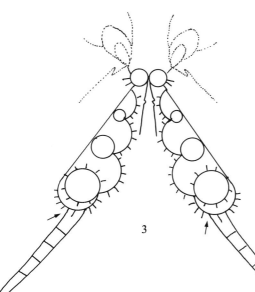

3

RW: 3rd Row: Ch: 4 + (1st P 1st Ch 2nd Row); 3 − 2 − 2 − 2 − 2 − 2 − 2 − 2 − 2 − 2 − 2 − 2;
RW: R: 7 + (7th P 1st Ch 2nd Row); 7; R Cl;
RW: Ch: 2 − 2 − 2 − 2 − 2 − 2 − 2 − 4 + (11th P 1st Ch 2nd Row);
Ch: 4 + (last P 2nd Ch 3rd Row); 2 − 2 − 2 − 2 − 2 − 2 − 2 − 4 + (6th P 2nd Ch 2nd Row), see 7.
RW: 4th Row: Ch: 5 + (1st P 1st Ch 3rd Row); 3 − 2 − 2 − 2 − 2 − 2 − 2 − 2 − 2 − 2 − 4 + (6th P 1st Ch 3rd Row); Ch: 4 + (9th P 1st Ch 4th Row); 2 − 2 − 2 − 2 − 2 − 4 + (5th P 2nd Ch 3rd Row);

To make the tail at the end of the wing, take the shuttle thread through 4th P of the loop marked * (see diag. 2) to the back of the work, approx. 60 cm. With shuttle on Th. 5 − 5 − 5 − 5 − 10 + (4th P); 5 + (3rd P); 5 + (2nd P); 5 + (1st P); 5; Th through 6th P to back of work and Fin, see 3.
The second wing is made the same as the first wing.

Upper wing
R: 7 − 2 − 2 − 2 − 2 − 2 − 2 − 7; R Cl, see 4.
1st Row: 1st Sh on 2nd Sh Th; 1st Ch: 7 + (1st P R); 2 − 2 − 2 − 2 − 2 − 2 − 2 − 2 − 2 − 2 − 2 − 2 − 2 + (last P R), see 5.
RW: 2nd Row: Ch: 2 − 2 − 2 − 2 − 2 − 2 − 2 − 2 − 2 − 2 − 2 − 2 − 4 + (6th P 1st Ch), see 6.
4 + (last P previous Ch 2nd Row); 2 − 2 − 2 − 2 − 2 − 2 − 2 − 2 − 2 − 2 − 2 − 4 + (11th P 1st Ch);

Ch: 4 + (last P 2nd Ch 4th Row); 2 − 2 − 2 − 2 − 2 − 2 − 2 − 2 − 5 + (5th P 3rd Ch 3rd Row), see 8.

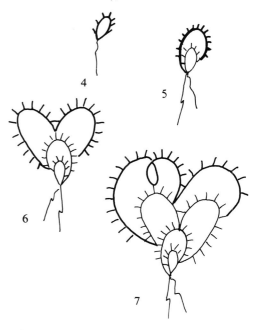

4

5

6

7

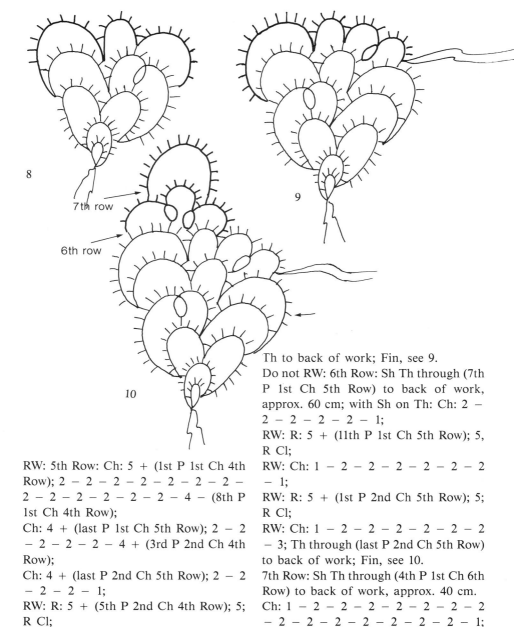

8

7th row

6th row

9

10

Th to back of work; Fin, see 9.

Do not RW: 6th Row: Sh Th through (7th P 1st Ch 5th Row) to back of work, approx. 60 cm; with Sh on Th: Ch: 2 − 2 − 2 − 2 − 2 − 1;

RW: R: 5 + (11th P 1st Ch 5th Row); 5, R Cl;

RW: Ch: 1 − 2 − 2 − 2 − 2 − 2 − 2 − 1;

RW: R: 5 + (1st P 2nd Ch 5th Row); 5; R Cl;

RW: Ch: 1 − 2 − 2 − 2 − 2 − 2 − 2 − 3; Th through (last P 2nd Ch 5th Row) to back of work; Fin, see 10.

7th Row: Sh Th through (4th P 1st Ch 6th Row) to back of work, approx. 40 cm.

Ch: 1 − 2 − 2 − 2 − 2 − 2 − 2 − 2 − 2 − 2 − 2 − 2 − 2 − 2 − 2 − 1;

Th through (2nd P 3rd Ch 6th Row) to back of work; Fin.

RW: 5th Row: Ch: 5 + (1st P 1st Ch 4th Row); 2 − 2 − 2 − 2 − 2 − 2 − 2 − 2 − 2 − 2 − 2 − 2 − 2 − 4 − (8th P 1st Ch 4th Row);

Ch: 4 + (last P 1st Ch 5th Row); 2 − 2 − 2 − 2 − 2 − 4 + (3rd P 2nd Ch 4th Row);

Ch: 4 + (last P 2nd Ch 5th Row); 2 − 2 − 2 − 2 − 1;

RW: R: 5 + (5th P 2nd Ch 4th Row); 5; R Cl;

RW: Ch: 1 − 2 − 2 − 2 − 2 − 2 + (3rd P 3rd Ch);

Second wing is made the same as the first. Join the wings at the points marked with arrows: diag. 3 (lower wing); diag. 2 (lower wing); diag. 10 (upper wing).

Body of the butterfly
Thread needle with wool. Use shuttle thread to make the knots. Leave approx. 4 cm of wool to attach antennae. Approx. 50 cm of the shuttle thread should be left (see diag. 11).

Ch: 3 – 2 – 2 – 2 – 22 – 22 – 2 – 2 – 2 – 3; slide knots close together (cotton is visible); cut shuttle thread approx. 50 cm long; thread into needle; keep wool threads together; cut together. Wind shuttle thread four times around the wool, from left to right and from top to bottom; thread left bead (see diag. 12), and attach antenna securely with the cotton, leaving a small space each fourth stitch; Fin (see diag. 13).

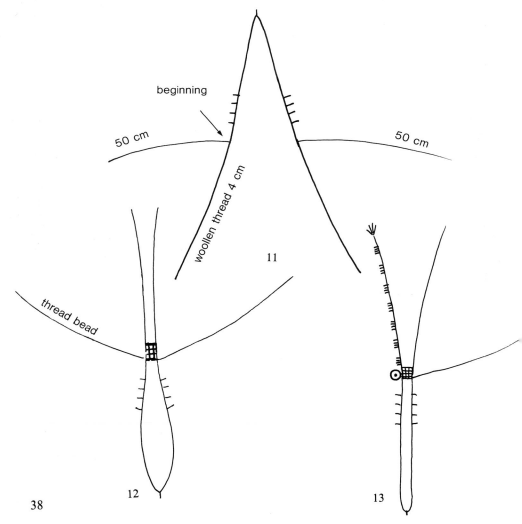

beginning

50 cm   50 cm

woollen thread 4 cm

11

thread bead

12

13

38

Photo 12   Butterfly. Instructions page 35

With the starting thread attach right bead; attach antenna similar to left antenna; Fin Th. With a fine needle and thread sew body together and attach the wings.

Mastering the elements of the art of tatting makes it possible to make the range of designs that have been part of the tatter's repertoire for many centuries, such as laces for decorating handkerchiefs, clothing and cushions and all sorts of doilies.

If you limit yourself to this traditional tatting you will find many books with instructions for this type of work. You may possibly find some variations on the old designs, but mostly in one colour. New dimensions in the art of tatting will be opened up to you in the following pages.

VI Tatting with a needle

Tatting has been practised for many centuries. Mostly it has been done with the aid of a tatting shuttle. The shuttle, however, has a double function. Firstly it is used to make the necessary knots and picots, secondly to keep the thread neatly rolled up. This last function was essential when making laces and doilies from one single colour cotton.

With much modern tatting, especially where several colours and very fine thread are used, it is preferable to use a needle rather than a shuttle. A long thread of the same sort and colour is not necessary for this sort of work, so there is no need to wind the thread around a shuttle.

Working with a needle has some advantages. In the first place the process of making a knot, especially for beginners, is a lot easier with a needle than with a shuttle. This is because you have to exert quite a lot of pressure on the left hand while making a knot with the shuttle. The loop needs to be held reasonably tightly around the four fingers of the left hand so that the shuttle can be passed through the loop before it can be passed back over the thread of the loop. Using a needle this can be accomplished in one easy movement.

Another advantage of working with a needle is that it opens up a whole range of new possibilities. Joins that would have been impossible to make with a shuttle can become a reality, thereby opening up an unlimited range of shapes. It also increases the variety of very fine cottons that you can use, thus increasing the number of colours that can be used. Using a needle is also less likely to damage the cotton, especially when using very fine cottons.

Knotting technique with a needle

The loop does not need to be around the whole of the left hand, but is held loosely around the thumb and forefinger and held in place lightly with the ring finger. The needle is passed partly under the loop (photo 13.1), then across the top and back under the working thread (this is the thread attached to the needle) (photos 13.2 and 13.3). The knotting thread 2 (looped thread) is slightly loosened (photo 13.4) and by pulling the working thread the knot is made (photo 13.5). Move the middle finger up to adjust the knot (photo 13.6). Hold the knot between the thumb and forefinger of the left hand and pass the needle over the knotting thread from top to bottom and pull through the loop (photos 13.7 and 13.8). Keeping the working thread taut, slide the knot with the middle finger against the previous knot (photos 13.9 and 13.10). If the thread starts to twist after making several knots, simply turn the needle between thumb and forefinger.

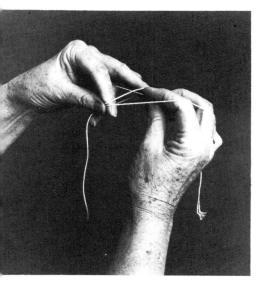

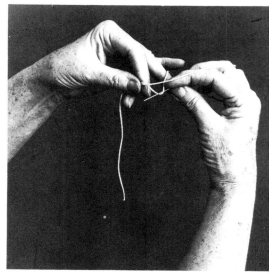

Photo 13.1 The needle is passed under the thread, which is held loosely between the forefinger and the middle finger

Photo 13.2 The needle is passed back across the top of the thread

Photo 13.3 With the thumb and forefinger of the right hand pull the needle back

Photo 13.4 The knotting thread is slightly loosened

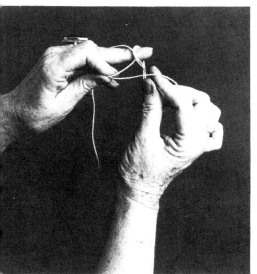

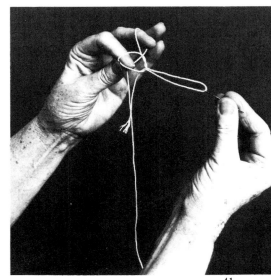

Colour photo 5 An attractive framed arrangement of small flowers, pansies and a bee

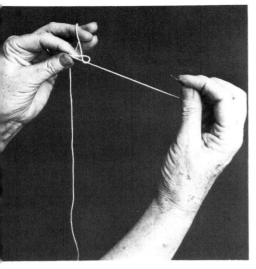 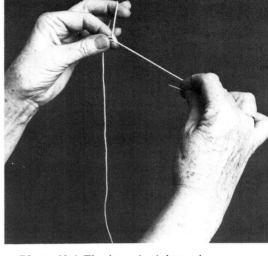

Photo 13.5 Pulling the working thread   *Photo 13.6 The knot is tightened*

Photos 13.7 and 13.8 Passing the needle over the knotting thread and pulling it through the loop to form the knot

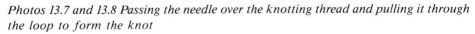

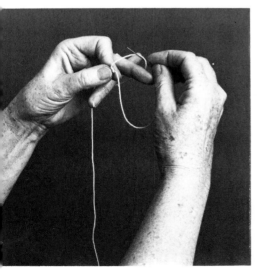 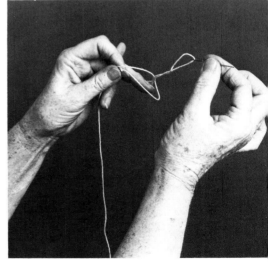

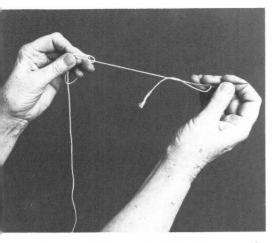
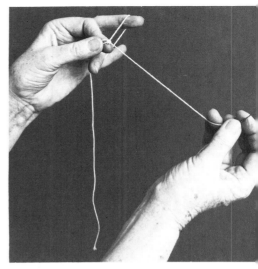

Photos 13.9 and 13.10 Tightening the thread and sliding the knot into position

Inverted tatting (working with two needles)
To make the following designs it is necessary to use two threads, making it necessary to use two needles. I recommend that you practise this first, preferably using a cotton that is neither too fine nor too slippery.

The working thread needs to be approx. 40 cm long; the knotting thread can be much longer. Holding the two threads together, between thumb and forefinger of the left hand, the knotting thread is passed down over the middle finger and held loosely by the other fingers. The knot is made in the same way as described previously. To prevent the working thread being pulled by the knots it may be advisable to thread a bead onto the beginning. Practising making the picots is very important: they need to be of equal size most of the time, although occasionally the patterns call for increasing or decreasing sizes.

This work consists mainly of rows going forward and returning, whereby the picots are joined to each other. The joining of the picots is one of the most important parts. After completing the desired number of picots alternated with double knots pull the knotting thread, with a needle or a crochet hook, through the last picot. This creates a new picot, through which the knotting thread is pulled (diag 14.1). The thread is tightened at the same distance from the first picot, so that after making a double knot, two picots have been created.

That it is not always necessary for the picot to be the same size as the picot to which it is to be joined is demonstrated in the following examples.

When the picots have been joined to one another, pull the joining knots once more by pulling the double knots on either side of the picots between thumb and forefinger and pulling the work into shape with both hands (diag. 14.2). This is especially important when making leaves and the wings of the dragonfly.

To join double knots, attach a needle to the knotting thread, pull this through the loop of the double knot and apply pressure till both knots are against each other—see the arrow in diag. 14.2.

If you wish to change to a different colour thread, after making a double knot pull the working thread over the middle finger and knot with the knotting thread over the working thread. The first half of the knot is now reversed. The knot can then be finished off as usual. Before changing colours make sure the knots have been slid into position—see diag. 14.4.

Diag. 14.1 The knotting thread in one piece is pulled through the newly formed loop

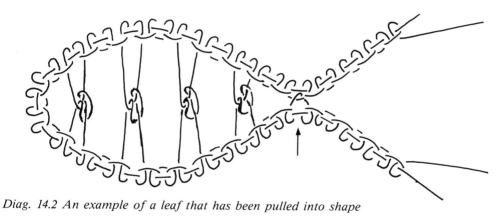

Diag. 14.2 An example of a leaf that has been pulled into shape

Diag. 14.3 Joining double knots

Diag. 14.4 Changing colours

VII Needle tatting

Once you have mastered the basics of needle tatting you can go on to start the rest of the designs in this book— butterflies, lizard, dragonfly and tropical fish. The Christmas angel is made mainly with a shuttle, but also requires the use of a needle. For the remaining designs only the needle is used, in conjunction with coloured cotton, as in the modern form of tatting.

The simpler designs are described first.

Christmas angel, see photo 9c (page 25)
Material: DMC Cotton no. 30 or 40, white; small beads
Equipment: 2 shuttles; needle; crochet hook no. 12
Method:
1st Sh; 1st R: 5 − 3 − 2 − 2 − 3 − 5; R Cl, see 1.
2nd Sh; thread 33 beads.
RW: 1st Sh on BS; Ch: 4 B 2 B 2 B 4, see 2.
RW: 1st Sh; R: 4 + (5th P 1st R); 2 − 2 − 2 − 2 − 4; R Cl, see 3.
RW: 1st Sh on BS; Ch: 3 B 2 B 2 B 3, see 4.
RW: 1st Sh; R: 3 + (4th P 2nd R); 2 − 2 − 2 − 2 − 3; R Cl, see 5.
RW: 1st Sh on BS; Ch: 2 B 2 B 2 B 2, see 6.
RW: 1st Sh; R: 2 + (4th P 3rd R); 2 − 2 − 2; R Cl, see 7.
With BS on 1st Sh; Ch: 5 − 4, see 8.
RW: With BS; R: 2 − 2 − 2 − 2 − 2 − 2; R Cl, see 9.
RW: With BS on 1st Sh: 4 + (P Ch); 5, see 10.

1st Sh; R; 2 − 2 + (2nd P 4th R); 2 − 2; R Cl, see 11.
RW: Ch, see 6.
RW: R: see 5, (middle P + middle P 3rd R); R Cl.
RW: Ch, see 4.
RW: 1st Sh; R: see 3, (middle P + middle P 2nd R); R Cl.
RW: Ch, see 2.
RW: 1st Sh; R: see 1, (middle P + middle P 1st R) R Cl, see 12.
RW: 1st Sh on BS; Ch: 3 B 2 B 2 B 2 B 2 B 2 B 3, see 13.
RW: 1st Sh; R: 3 + (last P last R); 3; R Cl, see 14.
RW: 1st Sh on BS; Ch: 2 B 2 B 2 B 2, see 15.
RW: 1st Sh; R: 3 + (P 1st R); 3; R Cl, see 16.
RW: 1st Sh on BS; Ch: 3 B 2 B 2 B 2 B 2 B 2 B 3, see 17.
Beginning and end threads are knotted together.

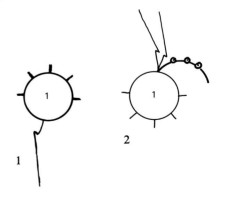

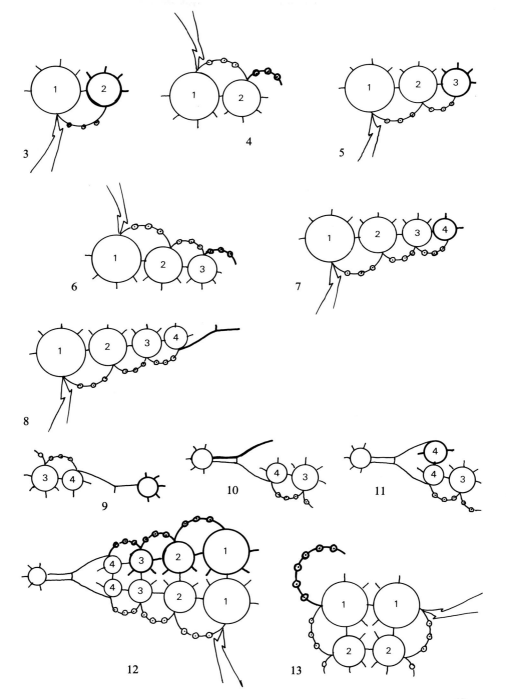

3

4

5

6

7

8

9

10

11

12

13

47

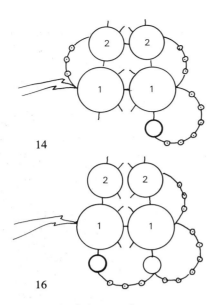

14

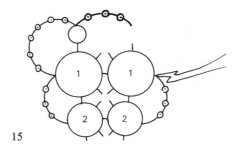

15

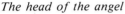

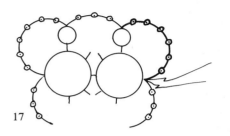

16

17

The head of the angel

1st Row: Sh Th is passed to the back between neck and ring, approx. 60 cm. Continue working shuttle on thread.

Ch: 1 − 1 etc. until you have made 29 picots, finishing with 1, pass shuttle to back of work, Fin, even picots with needle, see 18.

2nd Row: Sh Th through (4th P 1st Row), approx. 75 cm; thread 18 beads; work shuttle on bead thread.

Ch: * 1 B 1 − *, repeat from * to * till 18 beads are used; 1; thread through 25th P 1st Row; Fin, see 19.

Wing

1st Row: attach needle to shuttle thread; needle through bead picot of Ch (R1 to R2) approx. 100 cm. With needle on Sh Th; Ch: 2 − 2 − 2 − 2 − 2 − 2 − 2, see 20a.

With Sh; R: 6; R Cl.

With needle on Sh Th; Ch: 2 − 2.

With Sh; R: 6; R Cl.

With needle on Sh Th; Ch : 2 − 2.

With Sh; R: 6; R Cl.

With needle on Sh Th; Ch: 2 − 2 − 2 − 2. Pull the needle with the thread through 3rd P 3rd Ch (from 4th to 3rd R), Fin, see 20b.

2nd Row: thread 15 beads, needle through (1st P 1st Row), approx. 100 cm;

With needle on BS; Ch: 2 B 2 B 2 B 2 B 2 B 2 B 2 B 2 B 2.

BS; R: 6; R Cl;

Needle on BS; Ch: 2 B 2;

BS; R: 3 − 3; R Cl;

Needle on BS; Ch: 2 B 2.

BS; R: 6; R Cl;

Needle on BS; Ch: 2 B 2 B 2 B 2 B 2 B 2. Needle and thread through the starting point of the 4th R; Fin, see 20.

The second wing is made the same way as the first wing, this time starting at the top. The angel could be stiffened with starch or sugar water.

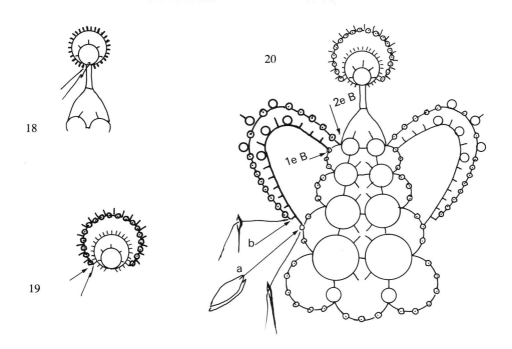

18

19

20

2e B

1e B

a

b

Mistletoe see photo 9d (page 25)
Materials: DMC cotton, green and cream
Equipment: 2 thin needles
Method:
Take a single thread approx. 70 cm long
and a single cream thread approx. 80 cm
long. Attach a needle to both threads.
The mistletoe is made using stems and
circular motifs to form the shape of the
flowers.
To make the stem use a cream thread and
knot this with the green thread: 15 DK.
With the cream thread make: R: 1 − 1 −
1 − 1 − 1 − 1; R Cl.
R (holding stem between left thumb and
forefinger) make a stem from 5 DK; R: 1
− 1 − 1 − 1 − 1 − 1; R Cl. With cream
thread; stem 3 DK; R, see 1.

The rings should be on the right hand side
of the green thread. Turn the last ring to
the left and make a stem of 3 DK.
Alternately, make some rings on either side
of the green thread—see diag. 2 and 3.
To get a realistic effect vary the flowers in
size. Use the same number of picots for
each flower, but vary the size of the picots
to vary the size of the flowers.
To make the branch look fuller, you can
occasionally attach the stem back to the
previous flower—see diag. 4. It may be
necessary to attach a new thread behind
a ring. When the branch is sufficiently big
finish off by knotting both threads
together. To make the leaves, take a single
green thread of cotton approx. 120 cm.
Pull needle and thread through the stem

at the top of the branch, approx. 25 cm (working thread)—see diag. 5. At the other end of the thread work the following; 5 – 2 – 2 – 2 – 2 – 2 – 2 – 2 – 2 – 9; the 1st and 9th picot are slightly smaller than the others—see diag. 6.

Attach a needle to the knotting thread and pull this through the 3rd knot from the end, till the knots are pushed against each other. 3 DK; picot is joined to 9th picot; 2 DK; joined to 8th picot. Repeat until all picots have been joined. 5 DK.

(N.B. The joining of picots is described on pages 44–45.)

Pull the needle with the knotting thread through the stem at the beginning of the leaf through the back of the work. Slightly pull working thread (see diag. 7) to pull the leaf up on a slight angle. Finish off. Don't cut threads but continue on to the leaf on the other side of the stem. Finish off and cut off threads.

By making more or less picots you can vary the size of the leaves. Continue making more leaves and finish off the branch to your own design—see diag. 8. These leaves can also be used to make other different branches.

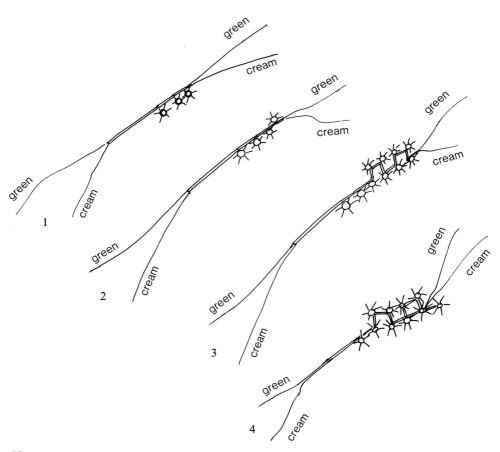

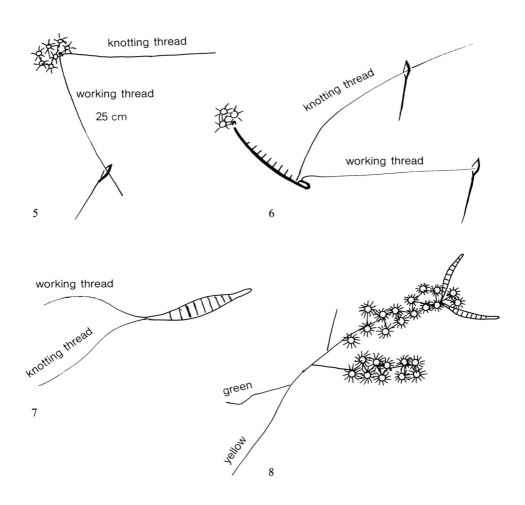

knotting thread

working thread

25 cm

5

knotting thread

working thread

6

working thread

knotting thread

7

green

yellow

8

Wattle, see photo 15a (page 52)
Material: Bright yellow cotton, green cotton
Equipment: 2 needles
Method:
Take a single green thread approx. 80 cm long and a single yellow thread approx. 80 cm long. Attach a needle to both threads. Work the same as for the mistletoe (see diag. 9d and description on page 49); make the first stem a little longer: 25 DK.

The yellow flowers are made from 12 picots alternated with double knots. The length of the picot determines the size of the flowers.

The side branches are made separately and then attached to the main stem, or can be attached to the main stem as described for the small daisies. The leaves are made the same and attached as for the mistletoe—see diag. 8.

51

Photo 15 a: Wattle, b: snowdrops, c: berry branches

Small daisies, see colour photo 1 (page 2)
Materials: DMC Cotton, white or pale pink, and light green
Equipment: 2 thin needles
Method:
Start by making a stem approx. 4 cm long (see instructions for mistletoe on page 49). The flowers are made of rings of 10 picots, slightly smaller than the wattle on page 51. Make alternating stems of 4 or 5 DK with one flower ring. The ring always stays to the right of the stem. Three rings form a group of flowers, and end with 4 DK—see diag. 1. The needle with the green thread is pushed through the back of the first stem, next to the first ring, then the threads are knotted together—see diag. 2. To start the second group of flowers, the needle with the green thread is pushed into

the stem approx. 0.75 cm below the first group, leaving approx. 16 to 18 cm of thread. The needle is worked on that piece of thread. The thread with the needle in it is longer. Make a stem of approx. 0.75 cm—see diag. 3. The pink thread is used to make a ring of 10 picots; keep this at the end of the stem—see diag. 4. With the pink thread make 4 DK on the longer green thread before the stem; continue: R; 4 DK; R; 4 DK. Finish threads off together at back of work.
The third group of flowers is made in the same manner—see diag. 5.
Finish off the branch by making several side branches attached to the main branch, and making groups of flowers of assorted sizes.

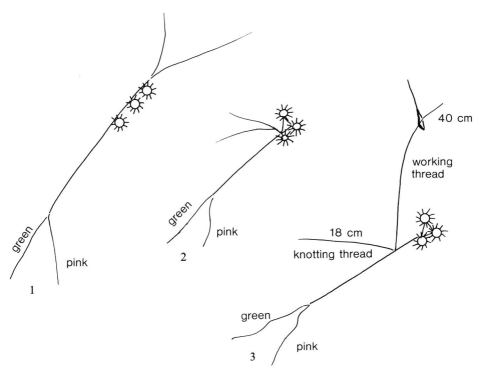

53

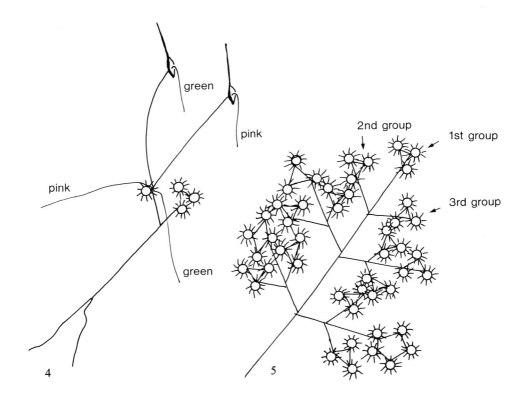

green

pink

pink

green

2nd group

1st group

3rd group

4

5

Rose 1, see photo 16a (page 57)
Material: DMC Cotton in 3 or 4 different shades of pink
Equipment: 1 needle
Method:
Thread needle with approx. 120 cm of cotton and make 5 rings as follows:
R: 7 − 2 − 2 − 2 − 2 − 2 − 2 − 7; R Cl.
The rings in the middle will fall against and over each other. Beginning thread and end thread are finished off together. These form the petals, see diag. 1 and 2. Each petal is now finished separately.
1st Row: needle with thread through 1st P, approx 25 cm; make a knot in the other end of the thread. The total length of the thread is approx. 75 cm, see diag. 3. Make 3 Ch.

1st Ch: 1 − 2 − 2 − 2 − 2 − 2 − 2 − 1. Needle through 3rd P.
2nd Ch as 1st; needle through 5th P.
3rd Ch as 1st; needle through 7th P to back of work and Fin, see diag. 4.
The next four rings are done in the same manner, using different shades of cotton.
2nd Row: is made from 4 chains; needle and cotton through 1st P of Row approx. 20 to 30 cm. Total length of thread approx. 100 cm.
1st Ch: * 1 − 1 − *, repeat from * to * till you have made 15 picots; 1. Needle through 5th picot.
2nd Ch make 17 P. Needle through (4th P 2nd Ch).

54

3rd Ch same as 2nd Ch. Needle through (3rd P 3rd Ch).

4th Ch same as 1st Ch, see diag. 5. Needle through last P to back of work and Fin. Repeat for the next four petals.

When the petals are finished, start to make the centre of the flower. Using a thread of approx. 100 cm (the knotting thread) and a thread approx. 25 cm (the working thread), attach a needle to both threads. Hold threads between thumb and forefinger and with the WT make 1 DK on the KT. With KT: approx. 0.5 cm from 1st DK: R: 10; R Cl, see diag. 6.

With WT make 1 DK on KT, 0.5 cm past R, slide against 1 st DK, see diag.7.

Keep repeating: R, DK.

By changing the length of the thread between the rings you'll achieve a more realistic effect—see diag. 8.

When the longer thread is finished, knot both threads together and pull through the middle of the rose to the back of the work. Afterwards, threads for both the rose petals and the centre of the rose are finished off together.

Instead of one centre for the rose, you could make two centres of different colours. You would then need to work with shorter lengths of thread, KT approx. 70 to 80 cm—see diag. 9 and 10.

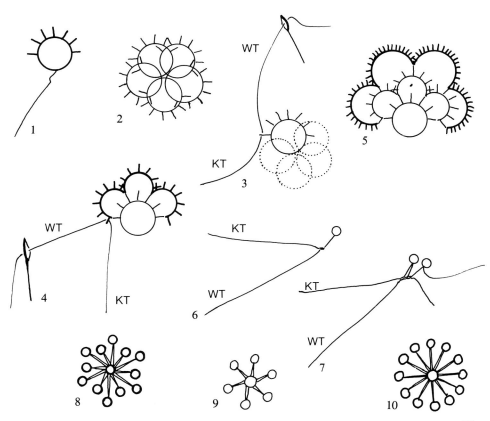

Rose 2, see photo 16b (page 57)

Material: DMC Cotton in 4 matching shades

Equipment: 1 thin needle

Method:

This rose is made with 5 petals. Start with 5 rings meeting in the middle. Length of thread approx. 85 cm. R: 5 − 2 − 2 − 2 − 2 − 5; R Cl, see diag 1.

Each petal is then finished separately.

1st Row: needle through (1st P R), WT 25 to 30 cm, total length 100 cm, see diag. 2. 1st Ch: 2 − 2 − 2 − 2 − 2 − 2 − 2 − 2 − 2 ; needle through 5th P R, see diag. 3. 2nd Ch: 5; P + (8th P 1st Ch) — see arrow in diag. 4 — (as described in chapter 4, 'Tatting with a needle'); 3 + (8th P 1st Ch); 3 + (7th P 1st Ch); 3 + (7th P 1st Ch). Continue working this way until picots 6, 5, 4 etc. are joined; 5; needle through (1st P R) through back of work, Fin, see diag. 4. To make the next row, take a thread approx. 80 cm; needle through (1st P R), see diag. 2.

3rd Row: 5; WT + (5th DK 2nd Ch) (see arrow in diag. 5); 2 − 2 − 2 − 2 − 2 − 2 − 2 − 1; WT + 2nd Ch (at 3rd R 1st Ch) see diag. 5.

Continue Row in the same manner, making another join at the 6th P 1st Ch with the 2nd Ch—up to the 5th DK before the end of the previous row.

WT joined to previous row, 5 DK, needle through last picot 1st R to back of work and Fin.

For the last row take a thread 90 to 100 cm, pull through last picot, i.e. (21st P 3rd Ch) (see arrow in diag. 6); 2 DK + 20th P; 3 DK + 20th P; 3 DK + 19th P, etc., see diag. 6.

When all picots have been joined pull needle through to back of work and Fin. To make the centre: see diag. 6, 7, 8, 9 and 10 for rose 1 (page 55).

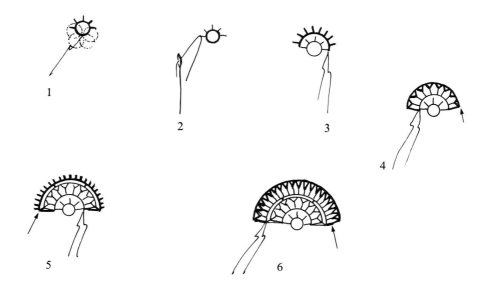

1

2

3

4

5

6

Photo 16   a and b: Roses; c and d: A variety of leaf shapes

Rose 3, see colour photo 2 (page 19)

Materials: Cotton in pale yellow and 5 different shades of salmon pink

Equipment: 1 thin needle

Method:

R: 5 − 2 − 2 − 2 − 2 − 5; R Cl (in pale yellow), see diag 1.

2nd Row: using a different colour, needle through 1st P; Ch: 3; + 2nd P, 3rd and 4th P are all joined with 3 P, alternated with 3 DK. The first and the last picots to be joined should be smaller than the others. End with 3 DK. KT through 5th P of the R to back of work and Fin, see diag 2.

3rd Row: using another colour, needle through 2nd and 3rd DK of 1st R (see arrow 1 in diag. 3). Ch: 5; WT + 2nd Row at arrow 2; 2 − 2 − 2 − 2 − 1; WT + 2nd Row; 1 − 2 − 2 − 2 − 2 − 1; WT + 2nd Row; 1 − 2 − 2 − 2 − 2; WT + 2nd Row; 5; WT + 1st R.

The length of the picots determines the shape of the petals.

4th Row; using another colour (see diag. 4); needle through last P 3rd Row (see arrow 3); 3; + following P; 3; + following P; 3; the next 2 P are each joined with 3 P alternated with 3 DK.

The next 3 following P + 1st P, alternated with 3 DK; following 2 P each + 3 P, the last 2 P joined with 1 P.

Finish with 3 DK; needle through last P and Fin.

The other 4 petals are made in the same manner. The first rows are made in pale yellow, changing the colours in the following rows so the petals will vary. The petals are joined together in the centre. Make the centres of the roses in different colours (see diag. 9 and 10 for rose 1, page 55) and attach these to the middle.

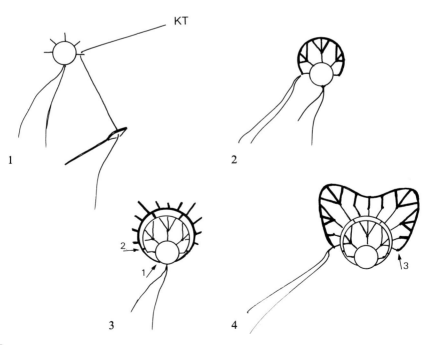

Colour photo 6   Frame with pansies

Pointed leaf, see photo 16d (page 57)
Materials: DMC Cotton, green
Equipment: 2 thin needles
Method:
In the first needle use 2 threads approx 40 cm long (working thread); in the second needle 1 thread approx. 130 cm. To make the stem make 2 cm DK; for the first leaf:
− 3 − 3 − 2 − 2 − 2 − 2 − 3 − 3 − 10; needle with KT through 3rd DK from last P, till knots become close together, see diag. 1.
Hold point of leaf between thumb and forefinger: 3 DK; P join to 9th (= last) P; 3 DK; P + 8th P; 3 DK; P + 7th P; 2 DK; P + 6th P; 2 DK; P + 5th P; 2 DK; P + 4th P; 2 DK; P + 3rd P; 3 DK; P + 2nd P; 3 DK; P + 1st P; 2 DK; needle with KT through 2nd DK past 1st P of stem;

3 DK; needle with KT through 5th DK, see diag. 2.
The second leaf sits next to the first leaf—see diag. 3. Commence with 5 DK and repeat as for first leaf. If the KT becomes too short, you will need to knot an extra thread here, to make the third leaf and stem.
The third leaf is made in the same manner as the second leaf. When the third leaf has been joined to the other leaves, finish the stem as follows: 5 DK; KT joined to the opposite 5th DK of the first half of the stem.
Repeat until both stems are the same length. The last join is made 3 to 4 DK before the end of the stem. Finish the 2 middle threads first, then the 4 outside threads.

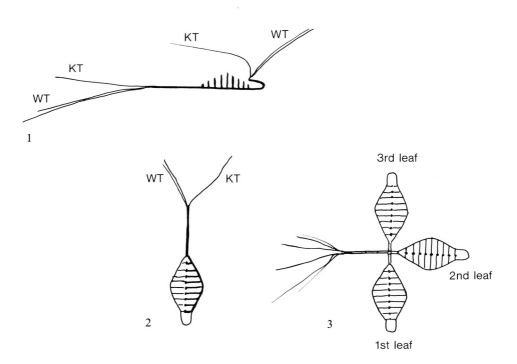

Round leaf, see photo 16c (page 57)
Materials: Cotton in two shades of green
Equipment: 2 thin needles
Method:
Thread both needles with a single thread of each green. The working thread is pale green and approx. 80 cm long, the knotting thread is dark green and approx. 100 cm long. Start with 15 DK, 6 P with 2 DK between each P. The two middle P are the longest, the next four P are made progressively smaller towards each end, see diag. 1.

4; + 6th P; 4 ; + 6th P; * 2 DK + 5th (etc.) P.
Repeat from * till all picots are joined. Needle with KT through 2nd DK from 1st P, see diag. 2.
Pull both threads gently, see diag. 3.

2nd Row: using the dark thread as WT: make approx 20 P with 2 DK between each P. After 7th and 14th P: WT joined to previous Row. Start by making a small picot and gradually increasing the size of the next 3 P; see diag. 4; then 12 P similar in size to the 4th, then 3 P becoming gradually smaller. 2 DK; WT joined to previous Row, see diag. 5.

3rd Row: change WT, 3 DK; + last P (the DKs close against the picots), see diag. 6.

As the picots become longer, make 4 DK between the P to be joined. When all picots have been joined, finish with 3 DK; + last DK 2nd row; 5 DK; + opposite DK from first half of stem, see diag. 7; repeat till both stems are the same size (join the last 3 or 4 DK before the end of the stem).

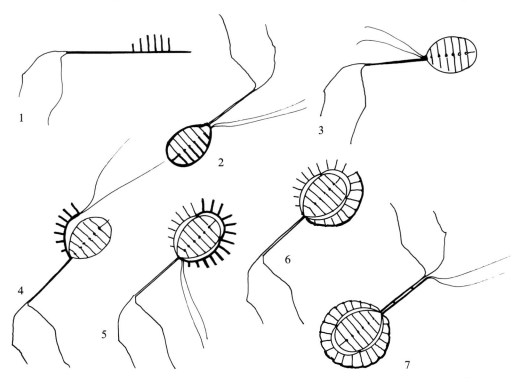

Lizard, see colour photo 8 (page 72)
Materials: 3 shades of green and 2 shades of blue cotton; 1 length of fine smooth silver or gold thread; small beads
Equipment: 2 needles
Method:

Body   The body is made up of 6 pairs of rings of 2 single threads, joined separately. Each pair is a different colour. The 3 middle picots of the first ring are larger than the other picots. This pair forms the head, see diag. 1.
The other picots are smaller so that the rings fit neatly against each other.
1st Row: 4 − 2 − 2 − 2 − 2 − 4; R Cl.
2nd Row: (against 1st Row): 4 − 4 − 4 − 4; R Cl; Fin.
First pair is now completed.
Second pair: R: 4 − 4 − 4 − 4; R Cl: 4 − 4; + P pair 1 (see arrow in diag. 1); 4 − 4; R Cl; Fin.
The 3rd, 4th and 5th pairs of rings are made from: 3 − 3 − 3 − 3, the 6th pair are made from 2 − 2 − 2 − 2, see diag. 2.

Tail   To make the tail, needle and cotton between 2 DK of the last ring (see arrow in diag. 2).
Ch: 3; P; 3; P; 12; attach needle to KT and join with the 4th DK from last P (see arrow in diag. 3); 3; KT through 2nd P; 3; KT through 1st P: 3; KT between 2 DK of last R (diag. 6) to back of work; Fin, see diag. 3.

Legs   Each leg is made from 2 R of 2 − 2 − 2 − 2, see diag. 4.
Make 4 legs.

Body   The body is worked with silver or gold thread. Thread a needle with two single threads of cotton (see 5). WT approx. 40 cm long, pull through the P of the last R (arrow 1, diag. 5). Holding the silver thread together with the WT, at the P make 8 DK; WT through (P following R 6). The double knots will need to be worked closely together.
All the side picots of the rings (6 up to and including 1) should be joined; as the distance between the picots varies in size make more or less double knots. Continue until lizard is shaped.

Head   The 3 picots of the head are not joined, around these make a chain of DK. When the last picot has been joined, continue to work on the tail as follows: 12; + tail piece (arrow 2, diag. 5); 15 + (end tail piece); 35; WT approx. 5 DK back through a DK (arrow 3, diag. 5); 15; + newly formed tail; 15; + end 1st tail piece. Continue finishing tail, once more + 1st tail piece ending at the 1st P of the last R. Finish threads, working silver thread to back of work and Fin.

Legs   For the left front leg, WT through silver edge (arrow 4, diag. 5) between 4th and 5th R (2 and 3 of diag. 2). Hold silver thread together with WT: 6 DK; WT through P of 1st leg-R; 5; WT through (side − P 2nd R); 8 − 8; WT through (2nd P 2nd R); 8 − 8; WT through (2nd P 2nd R); 8 − 8; WT through (3rd P 2nd R); 5; WT through (side − P 1st R); 3; WT through silver edge to back of work and after 4th R work back through the silver edge (arrow 5, diag. 5).
The other front leg is made in mirror reverse order. Finish off threads. The second pair of legs is attached to the 7th

and 8th R and worked in the same manner as the first pair of legs.

Eyes   The eyes are made of 1 R of 10 DK for each eye; do not cut WT; work silver thread around the eye and with the WT attach this twice to the circle, see diag. 6. With WT thread bead in centre of circle and attach eyes to the head, see diag. 5.

The lizard can be further embellished by fastening beads in the rings.

Fuchsia, see colour photo 3 (page 32)
Materials: Pale pink and purple cotton
Equipment: 2 needles
Method:

For the outer petals use two single threads of pale pink cotton approx. 90 cm long; thread one onto a needle and work as follows: 4: 16 times * – 2 *; after 16th P 9 DK; 17th P + 16th P; 2 DK; * – 2 *, repeat till all picots are joined; 4 DK; 2 KT are Fin. together. Adjust shape by pulling the WT; WT Fin together, see diag. 1.

To make the second outer petal thread a needle with the shorter thread and use the longer thread for knotting. 3 DK for the centre, continue as for the first petal. Attach needle to KT and pull through 4th DK at the beginning of the second petal (arrow, diag. 2); adjust petal shape; Fin, threads together, see diag. 2.

If the WT is long enough it can be used to make the third outer petal, using a new KT: 3; 16 times * – 2 *; 8; the following P + previous P; * 2 – *; continue knotting till all picots are joined; 3; needle through 3rd DK of the centre (arrow diag. 3) to back of work and Fin, see diag. 3.

With the same threads make the crown: 1 – 2 – 2 – 2 – 4; + 4th P; 4; + 4th P; 2; + 3rd P; 2; + 2nd P; 2; + 1st P; 1; needle through back of work; Fin, see arrow, diag. 4.

For the centre use 2 single threads of purple cotton of approx. 85 cm; thread one onto needle: 4 – 2 – 2 – 2 – 2 – 4; + 5th P; 4; + 5th P; 2 – 2 – 2 – 2 – 4; Fin Th, see diag. 5.

With the same WT make the following Row: 5; 13 P alternated with 2 DK, 4 times after a P joined to the 1st Row (see arrows, diag. 6), 5 DK; Fin Th.

For the last Row: attach a needle to the shorter thread; 6; P + (1st P previous Row); 3. The following P are joined with 2 P to the P of the previous Row, alternated with 3 DK. End with P + (last P previous Row); 6; Fin Th, see diag. 7. Attach centre behind the covering petals. To make an open fuchsia (see diag. 8), start by making petal no 1, then petal no 2, between petal 2 and 3 make 3 DK for the crown. Add petal no 4 and add the crown last, make the crown a little longer by starting with making 13P.

For the stamens, use 5 single threads pale pink cotton approx. 70 cm long. Pull half the thread through the back of the centre and knot the remaining half. For the middle stamen 2 cm (approx. 25 DK) with WT: R: 15; Fin Th, at back of R. Make the other stamen a little shorter with R of 10 DK.

The green leaves are made with two shades of green cotton. Take 2 single threads, thread one onto needle. Start with the calyx (flower base). The method is similar to the beginning of the centre: 3 – 2 2 – 4; + 3rd P; 4; + 3rd P; 2 – 2 – 3; Fin; 20; 15 P alternated with 2 DK (the loops are larger than for the flower petals); 9; thread second thread onto needle; + 3rd DK after 15th P; 2; change threads; 1; + 15th P; 2.

The next P are joined, alternated with 2 DK; some P are joined with 2 P; 4; + (4th DK from 1st P); take the longest thread as WT and with a new KT make second leaf, see diag. 9.

To assemble, attach the flower behind the leaves.

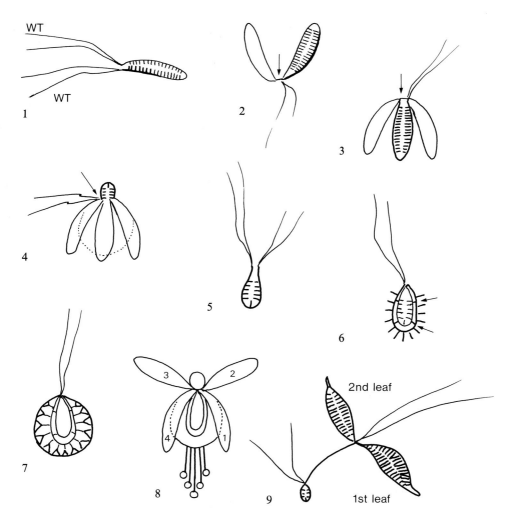

Snowdrops, see photo 15b (page 52)
Materials: White and green cotton
Equipment: 2 needles
Method:

The two covering petals are made the same as the outer petals of the fuchsia (see diag. 1 and 2), making 14 picots instead of 16 picots.

To make the centre use a green thread as the WT and a white thread as the KT.

Work in the same way as the fuchsia centre: 3 − 2 − 2 − 4; + 3rd P; 4; + 3rd P; 2 + 2 + 3; Fin Th, see diag. 2.

With the green WT make the next Row: 4 − 2 − 2 − 2 − 2 − 1; attach needle to white thread; join WT to previous Row; change WT; 1 − 2 − 1; join previous Row; change WT; 1 − 2 − 2 − 2 − 2 − 4; Fin Th.

Last Row with green WT: 5; + (1st P

previous Row); 3 + (2nd P previous Row); 3 + (3rd P previous Row); 3 + (4th P previous Row); 3 + (5th P previous Row). *Note:* the first two picots and the last two picots of this row will press against the joining picots. 1 DK; change WT; 2 + (5th P previous Row); 3 + (6th P previous Row); 2 ; Change WT; 1 + (6th P previous Row); 2 + (7th P previous Row); 1; change WT; 2 + (7th P previous Row); 3 + (8th P previous Row); 2; change WT; 1 + (8th P previous Row); 3 + (9th P previous Row); 3 + (10th P previous Row); 3 + (11th P previous Row); 3 + (12th P previous Row); 5; Fin.

Attach petals to centre of flower. To make the centre, pull needle with green thread through the DK 8th petal, see arrow, diag. 1.

1 – 2 – 2 – 2 – 2 – 4; + 4th P; 4 + 4th P; 2 + 3rd P; 2 + 2nd P; 2 + 1st P; 1; needle through back of work; Fin Th. Take neeedle and thread through back of centre, push up and make a small stem of

10 to 15 DK and attach to back of petal. To make a bud, make a third petal, see diag. 3.

After the flower, make the leaves of the snowdrop. Take 2 single strands of different shades of green cotton, 80 cm long.

Make the stem of 2 cm DK, continuing into the leaf: 19 times * – 2 *, making the first and last picots smaller than the others; 9 DK; thread the second needle; join the 3rd DK after 19th P; 2 DK; change WT; 1 DK; + 19th P; 2 DK; join all other picots * – 2 *; after last P: 3 + (opposite DK of stem); then every 5 DK: + stem.

When the stems are the same size Fin KT together. Pull leaf into shape and Fin WT together; see diag. 4; attach the flower behind the leaf.

The rest of the leaves are made in the same manner as the leaf attached to the stem, beginning with 4 DK and shaped from 25 P, see diag. 5.

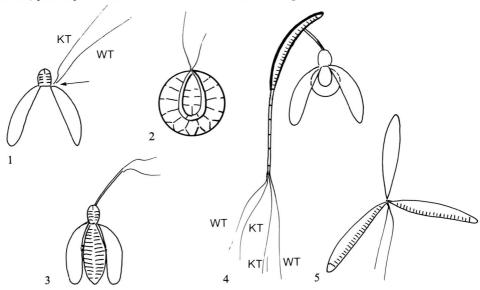

66

Dragonfly, see photo 11 (page 33)
Materials: 2 shades of pale blue or pale green cotton for the wings, brown cotton for the body; thin light brown wool for head and legs
Equipment: 2 needles
Method:

Wings Wings are made using 2 single threads as WT, 1 single thread as the KT: 9 – * 3 – *, repeat to make 21 P. (*Note:* the first 3 P are smaller than the others.) After the 21st P: 4 DK; 3 times * 4; P + 21st P *; continue: * 3 – *, repeat until 20 P are joined, ending with 9 DK, Fin, see diag. 1.

Using the same WT make the second wing the same as the first; Fin. Pull WT to shape the wing, see diag. 2.
With the same WT make the lower wings, using a different colour KT. Again making the first P slightly smaller than the others: 7 – * 3 – *, repeat from * to * to make 21 P; after the 21st P: * 4 + 21st P *; repeat twice; 3 DK; join the next 14 P as follows: * – 3 + *; the next 3 P each + 2 P, slightly longer than the previous; the last 3 P to be joined are smaller, continue 5 DK; Fin. Make the other wing mirror reversed, see diag. 3 and 4.

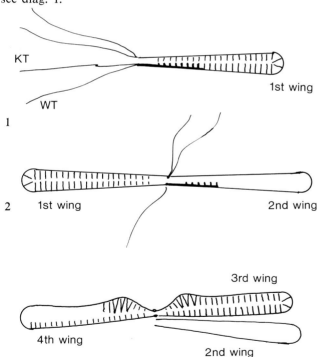

KT

1st wing

WT

1

2   1st wing   2nd wing

3rd wing

4th wing

2nd wing

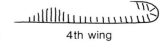

4   4th wing

67

Body For the body, see diag. 6: Using 2 single strands of brown cotton and 1 piece of thin light brown wool as WT: 5 – 5 – 5 – 5 – 5 – 5 – 5 – 25 – 5 – 5 – 5 – 5 – 5 – 5 – 5; fold over and attach together.

Head To make the head use 3 single threads brown cotton, making 2 rings each of 25 DK, see diag. 5.

The first R is pulled together in the centre (arrow 1, diag. 6); attach beads for eyes to the sides (arrow 2, diag. 6); the 2nd R is covered with threads (arrow 3, diag. 6); sew head and body together and attach to the wings.

Legs To make the legs use the same wool as used for the body. Use a single thread of cotton to solidly fasten the legs between the head and the body (see diag. 6).

Antennae The antennae are made in the same way. Attach between the two parts of the head (see diag. 6).

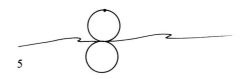

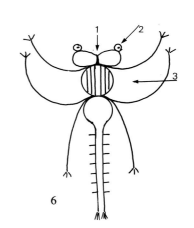

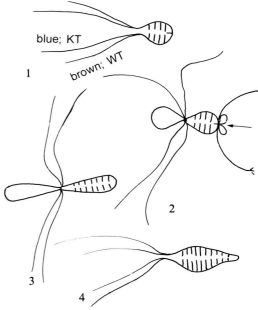

Fly, see colour photo 8 (page 72)
Materials: Blue, brown and 2 shades of light green or light blue cotton
Equipment: 1 needle
Method:

Body The body is made from 2 similar pieces, 5 – 2 – 2 – 2 – 4 + 4 + 2 + 2 + 2 + 5, beginning with blue KT (brown WT), see diag. 1.

When the work is finished knot the threads, then make the second part with the same threads against the first part (WT blue).

The unused threads are used to make the legs, see diag. 2.

Colour photo 7 Multicoloured butterflies

Head   To make the head, use the brown thread: R made from 18 DK. Attach together in the centre and sew to the body (arrow, diag. 2). Fin. threads and fasten off.

Lower wings   To make the lower wings: 5 – 2 – 2 – 2 – 2 – 2 – 2 – 8; working back, join the picots; 5; Fin, see diag. 3.
Make the 2nd lower wing, using the same WT as the first wing.

Upper wing   For the upper wing: 5 – 2 – 2 – 2 – 2 – 2 – 2 – 2 – 2 – 8; working back join picots; 5; Fin, see diag. 4. Make the 2nd upper wing using the same WT.

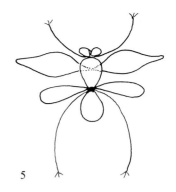

Attach wings behind body. To make the legs, take an extra thread of cotton and loop it around from the centre to the desired length, see diag. 2.

Bee, see colour photo 8 (page 72)
Materials: Orange and brown cotton, 2 small beads
Equipment: 1 needle
Method:
Using brown WT and orange KT: 1 – 2 – 2 – 2 – 2 – 2 – 2 – 2 – 7; working back join the picots; 6; pull WT to correct shape, see diag. 2; Fin, see diag. 1 and 2

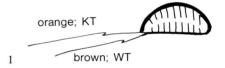

RW: with orange WT 2 – 2 – 2 – 2 – 2 – 2 – 2 – 2; in the centre and at the end WT is joined to previous Row; 6 DK; + 7 P, 6 DK: needle to back of work; Fin, see diag. 2.

RW: needle with brown thread through 6th DK (arrow 1, diag. 3): 3 – 2 – 2 – 2 – 2 – 3; + 6th DK last Row; 4 DK; + 5 P; 4 DK; needle to back of work; Fin, see diag. 3.
The threads can be stitched on later for the legs.

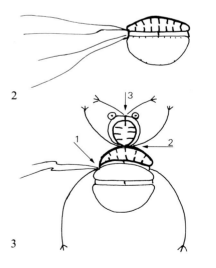

Head To make the **head**, take needle with brown thread and stitch through the top of the body (arrow 2, diag. 3); 2 – 2 – 2 – 4; + 3rd P; 4; + 3rd P; 2 – 2 – 2; needle to back of work; Fin.

WT: 2 small beads; make a row of DK around the head. The beads form the eyes. Threads are Fin. and then sewn around for the legs. Use a doubled thread to stitch through the head and fasten into position. (arrow 3, diag. 3).

Wings The wings are made the same as in diag. 3 and 4 for the fly—the lower wing 9 P, upper wing 13 P.

To make the other legs pull a piece of thread through the body and fasten into position.

Rose 4, see colour photo 2 (page 19)
Materials: 4 shades of pink cotton
Equipment: 2 needles
Method:
The centre of the rose is made from the darkest shade. As the petals get larger, they become lighter in colour. The first 3 petals are made the same size. Use a single thread and start by making R: 5 – 2 – 2 – 2 – 2 – 2 – 2 – 5; Fin. For the second Row use a new thread (KT). For both the first and second Rows the 1st picots are smaller than the remaining picots, see diag. 1.

2nd Row: 6; P + (1st P 1st Row); 3; P + (1st P 1st Row);
* 3; P + (2nd P 1st Row); 3; P + (2nd P 1st Row); 3; P + (2nd P 1st Row)*.
Repeat from * to * joining the picots of the first Row; the last P same as the first; ending with 6 DK; Fin, see diag. 2. Roll petals and fasten off; cut Th.
When the first 3 petals have been attached

to each other, make the following 2 petals larger by 2 Rows, see diag. 3 and 4.
3rd Row: 7; – 2 – 2. Continue, ending with 7 DK.
4th Row: 8; + 3 + 3; 2 times (+ 3); + 3; etc., ending with 8 DK; Fin.
By varying the length of the picots, the sizes of the petals can be varied; the number of P that need to be made depends on the size of the first petal. By pulling the WT slightly the last petals can be curled around.

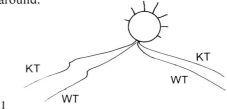

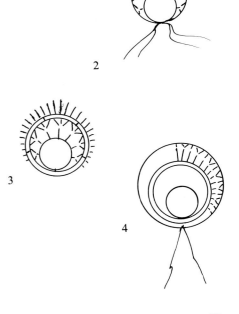

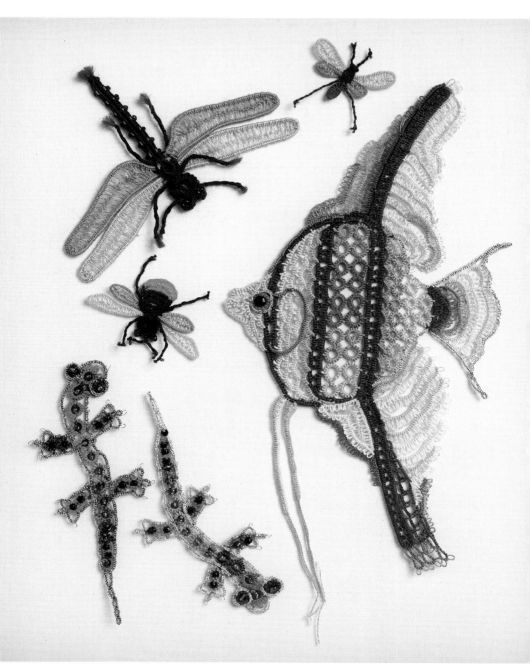

Colour photo 8 A tropical fish, dragonfly, fly, bee and lizards

Forget-me-not, see colour photo 1 (page 2)
Materials: Blue and green cotton
Equipment: 2 needles
Method:
Use a single thread of each colour. With the needle begin with the green stem, making a section 2.5 cm long, see diag. 1; for the flower, with blue cotton, make R of 6 P alternated with 1 DK; 3 DK, join 3rd DK from R (arrow 1, diag. 1). Stem 2 cm; R: 3 DK, R: 3 DK, R: 3 DK; join 1st R (arrow 2, diag. 1); 4 DK join stem (arrow 3, diag. 1); stem 1.5 cm; group of 6 R; 3 DK join to 1st R of group; 5 DK join stem (arrow 4, diag. 1). Continue working spray as diag. 2.

To make the leaves, use the directions for the mistletoe on page 49, approx. 11 P, see diag. 2.

To make the berries use the same method; the berries are attached to the spray, some with stems. The berries are made from R 11 to 12 DK, see diag. 3.

The sprays can have leaves if you wish; use the directions for the mistletoe or wattle (pages 49 or 51).

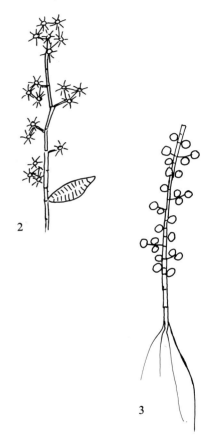

2

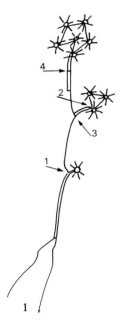

1

3

The remaining pieces do not have detailed descriptions; instead follow the directions on the diagrams. The numbers on the diagrams indicate the numbers of DK required. When making the butterflies, work totally to the diagram.

Violets, see colour photo 2 (page 19)

Materials: Yellow cotton and 4 shades of blue cotton

Equipment: 2 needles

Method:

To make the first petal, use a single thread of light blue cotton threaded in the needle (WT). KT: 1 single thread yellow cotton: R: 3 − 2 − 2 − 4 − (+ 3rd P) 4 − (+ 3rd P); 2 − (+ 2nd P); 2 − (+ 1st P); 3; − R Cl; Fin. With yellow WT; 5 − 2 − 2 (join to 1st R); − 2 − 2 − 2 − 2 − 2 − 2 (join to 1st R); − 2 − 5; −(see arrow, diag. 2); Fin, see diag. 1 and 2.

With light blue: thread and needle through 3rd DK previous Row (arrow, diag. 3). Finish R as shown diag. 3, i.e.

3 + (1st P previous Row); 3 + (2nd P previous Row);

3 − (+ 3rd P previous Row); 3 − (+ 3rd P previous Row)

3 − (+ 4th P previous Row); 3 − (+ 4th P previous Row);

3 − (+ 4th P previous Row); 3 − (+ 5th P previous Row);

3 − (+ 5th P previous Row); etc., see diag. 3.

For the second petal, use two different shades of blue; start as for petal 1 (but use 9 P), see diag. 4. 2nd Row: same WT and a different shade of blue, continue working as diag. 4.

For the third petal, see diag. 5: 4th shade of blue, begin with 11 P, continue working as diag. 5. Make two each of the second and third petals, changing colour as desired.

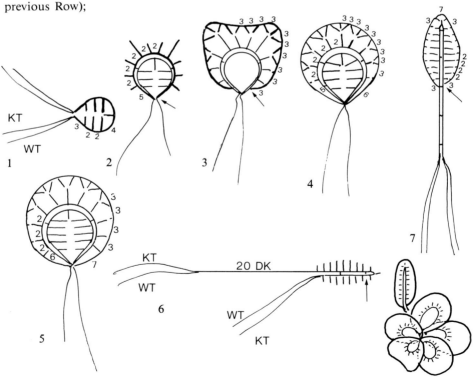

Attach petals to each other, see photo page 42. The green leaves are made in two shades (see diag. 6 and 7). Change WT for the second row.

Leaves for the roses and all the other leaves can be made in the same way.

Pansies, see colour photo 2 (page 19)

Materials: 5 or 6 different coloured cottons, colours as desired

Equipment: 2 needles

Method:

The starting rings cf all 4 flower petals are made in orange. Three petals are the same in shape and size, but vary in colour.

To start, see diag. 1: 3 − 2 − 2 − 4 + 4 + 2 − 2 − 3; R Cl; continue working as detailed in diag. 1.

For the first row take 1 thread of a different colour, begin at the arrow in diag. 1.

Second row, see diag. 2, work with the longest thread as WT and a new KT of a different shade (arrow 1, diag. 2). When joining picots 3, 4 and 5 keep changing the WT.

Third row, using a new KT, begin at arrow 2, diag. 2, approx. 24 P (depending on the size of the previous row).

Fourth row, as diag. 3. Thread to back of work and Fin.

Petal is now completed, see diag. 3.

The next three petals (petals 2, 3 and 4) are made using different shades of cotton; work according to directions in diag. 1, 2 and 4. These petals are made in a slightly more rounded shape by making the centre joining picots of the last row a little larger, see diag. 4.

Petal 5, see diag 5.

Attach petals 2 and 3 on either side of petal 4, petal 5 behind petals 4 and 3, petal 1 in front of petals 2 and 3.

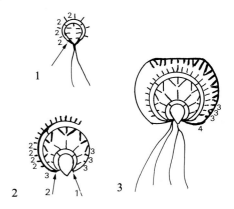

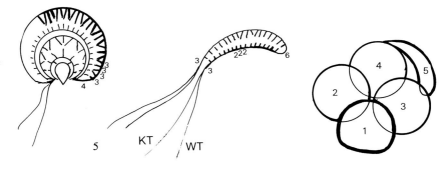

Butterflies, see colour photo 7 (page 69)
Butterflies are rewarding projects in tatting. Detailed descriptions are included here. A word of warning! Perhaps you will discover while you are working that, even though you have followed the description carefully, your design has a rather different shape. The number of picots and double knots prescribed is not always exact. A lot depends on the materials being used, the size of the picots that have been made and how tightly the double knots have been pushed along the threads. It may be advisable before you start to make a sketch of the butterfly (you could trace the example). You would then be able to compare your work with it as you go along. If your butterfly should turn out to be not exactly the same as the example, it really does not matter. Your design will have a unique beauty all its own.

Butterfly 1, see colour photo 7 (page 69). The first butterfly is made in pink and lilac shades with gold or silver thread for added interest. The edges of the wings and the body are black. The forward-worked picot rows are alternated with 2 DK. The return joining rows are alternated with 3 DK, except for the last row. A different shade of cotton could be used for each row.

Lower wing
Start with 2 rings, leaving enough room to fit the body between, see diag. 1.
1st Row: needle and thread through 1st R (arrow 1, diag. 2) 4 DK; join picots; 4 DK; see diag. 2.
To keep the wings even in size, after working a row on the right wing, work a row on the left wing in the opposite direction, see arrow 2, diag. 2.
2nd Row: see diag. 3: using the same WT and silver KT: 9 DK (arrow 1, diag. 3).
3rd Row: needle and thread through 2nd Row (arrow 2, diag. 3).
For this and the following rows, the number of DK at the beginning and end and between the picots is determined by the size and shape of each previous row.
4th Row: see diag. 4: needle and thread through P (arrow 1, diag. 4).
5th Row: start with silver thread (arrow 2, diag. 4).
6th Row: use black thread (arrow 3, diag. 4).

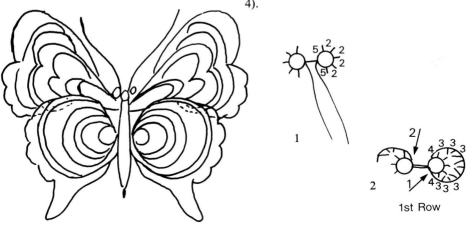

1st Row

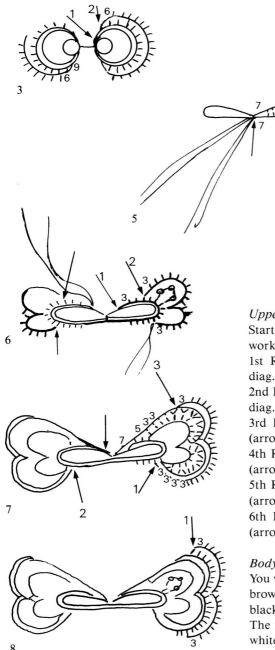

Upper wing

Start at (arrow, diag. 5). Both wings are worked at the same time.

1st Row: needle through DK (arrow 1, diag. 6).

2nd Row: needle through 3rd P (arrow 2, diag. 5).

3rd Row: needle and thread through P (arrow 1, diag. 7).

4th Row: needle and thread through DK (arrow 3, diag. 7).

5th Row: needle and thread through DK (arrow 1, diag. 8).

6th Row: needle and thread through P (arrow 1, diag. 9).

Body, see diag. 10

You will need to use 1 thread of thin light brown wool (WT) and 2 single threads of black cotton (KT) and 2 beads.

The instructions are the same as for the white butterfly on page 35.

77

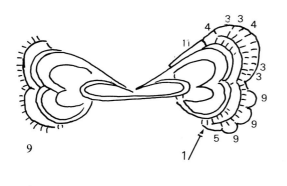

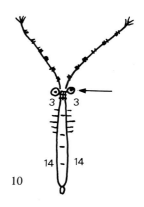

9 1 10

Butterfly 2, see colour photo 7 (page 69) This is made in the same manner as butterfly 1, but the upper wing has an extra row of picots, alternated with 1 DK. The opening created in the upper wing between rows 1 and 2 could be filled with rings, with or without beads. The colours are pale yellow, pale yellowish green, sand, yellowish brown and a soft brown.

Butterfly 3, see colour photo 7 (page 69) Made in shades of turquoise, green and blue, following directions (diag. 1 and 2). The 'eyes' in the lower wings are formed by making a ring of 9 picots in orange, surrounded by a row of blue DK, see diag. 3. Attach these to the wings (arrow 7, diag. 2). The last row of the wing is worked around the eye. The small ring at the lower end of the wing is made from 10 DK. The body: 1 thread of light brown wool (WT) and 2 single threads of brown cotton.

To make the eyes use 2 beads, see diag. 4. Attach the body to the wings.

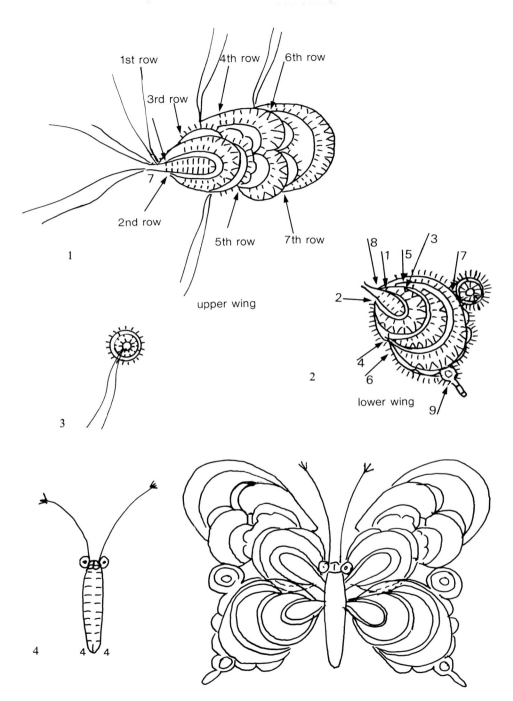

1st row
3rd row
4th row
6th row

7

2nd row

5th row
7th row

1

upper wing

8
1
5
3
7

2

4
6

9

lower wing

2

3

4

4 4

79

Butterfly 4, see colour photo 7 (page 69) This lemon butterfly is made in natural colours. The lower wing is in pale green pastel shades, going into pale yellow. The upper wing gradually becomes yellow, see colour photo.

The wings are made in parts. Begin with part 1, see diag. 1. Work a row of DK in cream around the edge.

Parts 2 and 3 are edged with DK in the same way.

Continue with parts 4, 5, 6, 7 and 8, working a row of DK around part 5 only, see diag. 2.

To finish work 3 rows of picots and 1 row of DK (arrows 1 and 2, diag. 3).

The upper wing is made following diag. 4 and 5.

To make the body use 2 times 2 single threads of light brown cotton. For the antennae and front legs, pull a double thread through the head and the body and work around. The back legs are formed using the leftover WT, see diag. 6.

The small space between parts 2, 3 and 4 of the lower wing are filled with a ring made of 10 DK in a rust brown colour.

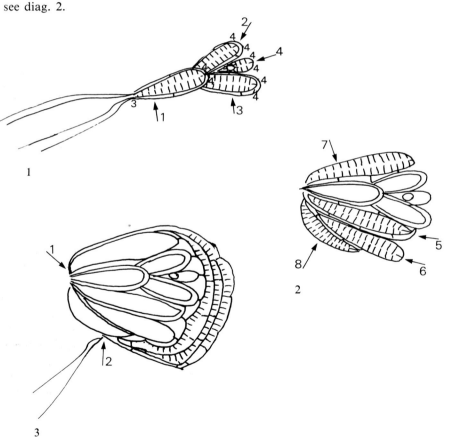

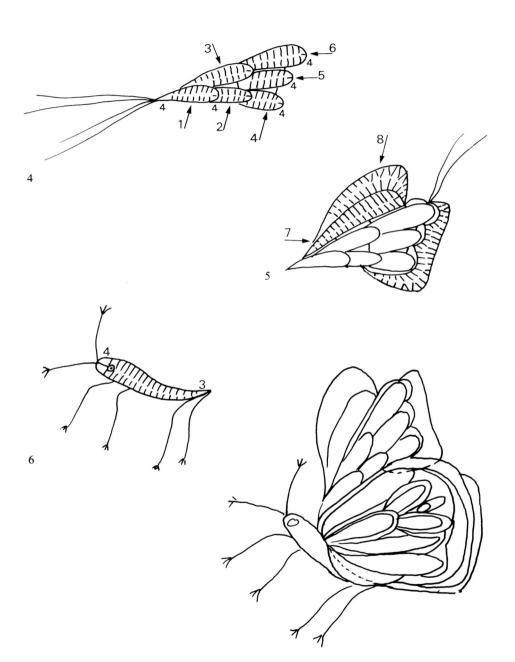

4

3

6

4

5

4

4

1

4

2

4

4

8

7

5

4

3

6

81

Butterfly 5, see colour photo 7 (page 69)
Begin by making two joined rings with a row of picots around them, see diag. 1.
Each wing is then finished separately, using mainly rows of forward-going picots. The few returning rows of joined picots can eventually be substituted by forward-going rows.
The rows of picots are alternated with 2 DK, the picots of the outside row being alternated with 1 DK.
Make the lower wings in the same manner, following diag. 2.

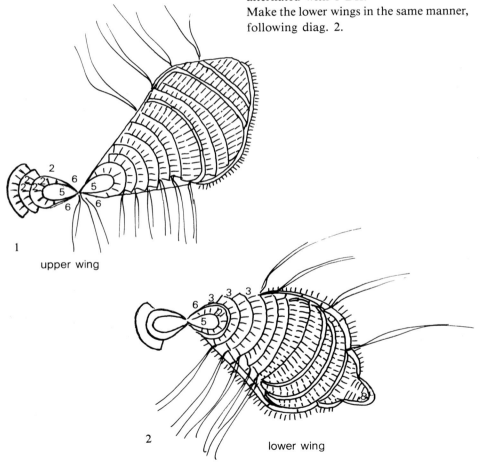

upper wing

lower wing

Tropical fish, see colour photo 8 (page 72)
Material: Cotton in colours of your choice
Equipment: 2 needles
Method:
The body of the fish, except for the fins, is made from 2 single threads of cotton. Start with 10 times 2 R of 4 − 4 − 4 − 4, which are joined separately. Work following the numbers, see diag. 1.

1st forward and returning Row; needle and thread through P of R 18 (arrow 1, diag. 1), through to (arrow 3, diag. 1), Fin.

2nd Forward Row; (arrow 2 diag 1 to arrow 3, diag. 1) Fin.

Returning Row: (arrow 4, diag. 1 to arrow 5, diag. 1) Fin.

3rd Row: (arrow 1, diag. 2); 5 DK + (DK previous Row); 2 − 2 − 2 − 1; join previous Row. Eight times 1 − 2 − 2 − 2 − 2 − 1; join to previous Row; last Ch 1 − 2 − 2 − 4; join to previous Row; Fin, see diag 2.

4th Row: (arrow 2, diag. 2); start (1st P 3rd Row); 2 − 2 − 2 − 2 − 2 − 2 + (P 3rd Row); seven times 2 − 2 − 2 − 2 − 2; last Ch 2 − 2 − 2 − 3; + (3rd P 3rd Row); Fin.

5th Row: (arrow 3, diag. 2); start with 3rd P 4th Row: 3 − 2 − 2 − 2 + (Ch 4th Row); six times 2 − 2 − 2 − 2; last Ch 2 − 2 − 2 − 3; + (2nd P last Ch 4th Row); Fin.

6th Row: (arrow 4, diag. 2); start 2nd P 5th Row: six times 2 − 2 − 2 − 2; last Ch 2 − 2 − 4; + (2nd P last Ch 5th Row); Fin.

7th Row: (arrow 5, diag. 2); start (2nd P 1st Ch 6th Row): 6 DK + (2nd P 2nd Ch 6th Row); three times 3 − 3; + (2nd P 5th Ch 6th Row); 6 DK + (2nd P 6th Ch 6 th Row); 6 DK + (2nd P 7th Ch 6th Row); 6 DK + (P 5th Row); 6 DK + (P 4th

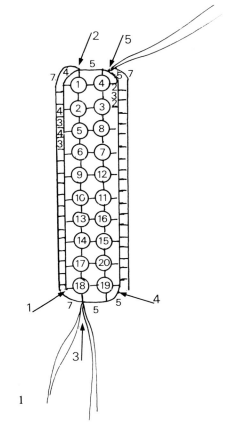

Row); 7 DK + (3rd DK before arrow 2, diag. 1).

7th returning Row: (arrow 6, diag. 2): 6 DK + previous Row, 5 DK + previous Row; 6 DK + P previous Row; 6 DK + P previous Row; 6DK + P previous Row; 6 DK + DK previous Row; 6 DK + previous Row; 6 DK + previous Row ; 10 DK + previous Row; 8 + DK 3rd Row; Fin.

The mouth 1st Row: (arrow 7, diag. 2); 3 − 2 − 2 − 2 ; + previous Row; 2 − 2 − 2 − 2; + previous Row; 3rd Ch as

2nd Ch; + previous Row; 2 − 2 − 3; Fin, see diag. 2.

2nd Row: (arrow 8, diag. 2): 2 − 2 − 2 − 2 ; + previous Row; 2 − 2 − 2 − 2; + previous Row; 2 − 4; + previous Row; 5 DK; + (last P previous Row). Complete as shown in diagram.

Back section of body 14 R: 3 − 3 − 3 − 3; work in number order, see diag. 2.

1st Row: (arrow 9, diag. 2); 3 − 2 − 2; + previous Row; 2 − 2; + 1st R; 2 − 2; + previous Row.

Continue working this way until all 8 R are joined; Fin.

Tail fin (Arrow 10, diag. 2): 5 DK; join; 2 − 2 − 2; join; 5 DK; join.

2nd Row: returning; 3 DK; join; 4 DK; + P; 3 DK; + P; 4 DK; join; 3 DK; join; Fin. The next 5 rows of picots are alternated with 2 DK (as diagram). Around these make a row of DK from arrow 11 (broken line) making a beginning and ending picot as in the diagram.

For both the upper and lower fin (see diag. 3) the middle is made from a forward-going and returning Row of 2 single threads (as diagram). The P rows of the fins are alternated with 2 DK and made as shown in the diagram.

The second forward and returning Rows of the lower fin are made from a single thread.

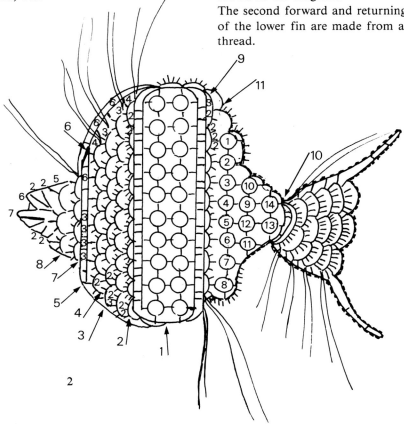

The feelers are made from a single thread and started at the stomach. (Arrow 12); 3 − 3 − 3 − 3, approx 7 cm. Returning Row starts at arrow 13.

To make the eye, make a R of 15 DK knotted around with silver thread, and a bead in the centre.

For the gill use a single thread, see diag. 3.

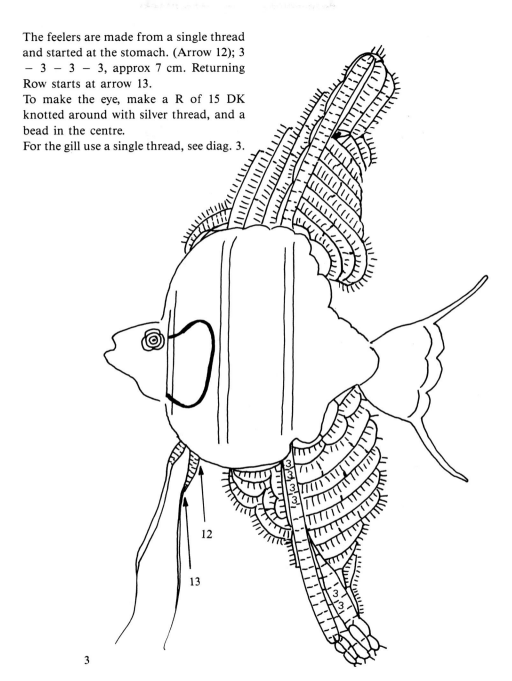

VIII Conclusion

A number of the projects in this book are suitable for framing as attractive wall or window decorations. Not large objects obvious at first glance, nonetheless they have their own characteristic small-scale beauty.

Suitable frames are available in most craft shops and can be bought in many shapes and sizes.

Start by working around the edge of the frame. This can be done either by using a crochet hook with a blanket stitch, or with tatting knots.

Embroidery cotton or mercerised cotton will give the best result. The choice of material and colour will depend on the design to be used in the frame. In most cases complementary toning colours will give a more pleasing effect than very strong contrasting colours, although some very interesting effects can be achieved with contrasting colours. It is really a question of personal taste.

Attaching the design to the frame can be done in different ways. The best way is to make a background with a blanket or other type of stitch, see diag. 17. Attach the design to this background. Several completed frames appear in the book. Many other combinations are possible, so use your imagination to make anything you like. You could also use silk or handpainted fabric as a background for the butterflies, in natural colours, combined with branches, leaves or flowers. This will also depend on your taste.

There are many other possible ways of using tatting. You could use it to trim your clothes or make brooches or necklaces from the pansies or roses, for example. Those people who like to make their own greeting cards could use the designs on page 49, such as the mistletoe, for Christmas cards. The wattle and berry branches, the fuchsias and snowdrops, would be perfect for this (pages 51, 64 and 65). We wish you every success in making the coloured tatting.

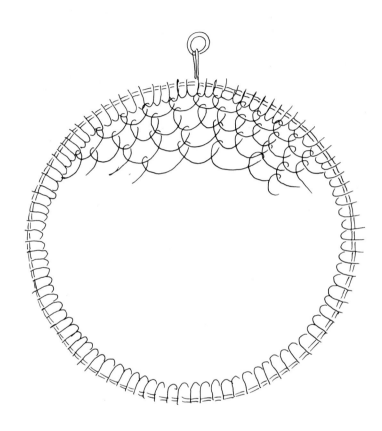

Diag. 17   Frame with edge and background made up of blanket stitches